Strategic Software Engineering

Software Engineering Beyond the Code

Filipe Ximenes

Apress®

Strategic Software Engineering: Software Engineering Beyond the Code

Filipe Ximenes
Recife, Pernambuco, Brazil

ISBN-13 (pbk): 979-8-8688-0994-1   ISBN-13 (electronic): 979-8-8688-0995-8
https://doi.org/10.1007/979-8-8688-0995-8

Copyright © 2024 by Filipe Ximenes

Managing Director, Apress Media LLC: Welmoed Spahr
Acquisitions Editor: James Robinson-Prior
Development Editor: James Markham
Coordinating Editor: Gryffin Winklerv

Cover image designed by Freepik (www.freepik.com)

Illustrations designed by Pedro Barcelar and Jason Santos

Distributed to the book trade worldwide by Springer Science+Business Media New York, 233 Spring Street, 6th Floor, New York, NY 10013. Phone 1-800-SPRINGER, fax (201) 348-4505, e-mail orders-ny@springer-sbm.com, or visit www.springeronline.com. Apress Media, LLC is a California LLC and the sole member (owner) is Springer Science + Business Media Finance Inc (SSBM Finance Inc). SSBM Finance Inc is a **Delaware** corporation.

For information on translations, please e-mail booktranslations@springernature.com; for reprint, paperback, or audio rights, please e-mail bookpermissions@springernature.com.

Apress titles may be purchased in bulk for academic, corporate, or promotional use. eBook versions and licenses are also available for most titles. For more information, reference our Print and eBook Bulk Sales web page at http://www.apress.com/bulk-sales.

Any source code or other supplementary material referenced by the author in this book can be found here: https://www.apress.com/gp/services/source-code.

If disposing of this product, please recycle the paper

To Isadora, Regina, Marcos, and Rafael

Table of Contents

About the Author

Filipe Ximenes was born and raised in Recife, a city in the northeast of Brazil renowned for its rich historical and cultural heritage and thriving tech industry. He is one of the founders of Vinta Software (`https://www.vintasoftware.com/`), a software development shop that specializes in partnering with clients to build and maintain successful products using modern tools and proven practices. For over a decade, Filipe has managed teams and built products at various stages of maturity, from writing the first line of code as the sole engineer on a project to seamlessly integrating full squads into established teams. An avid believer in the power of openly sharing knowledge, Filipe was drawn early in his career to his local Python programming community. Since then, he has created and collaborated on numerous open source projects, organized conferences, and given talks at major events in Brazil, the United States, Europe, and Australia.

About the Technical Reviewer

 Rafael Carício is a Senior Software Engineer at Netflix, currently part of the Live Streaming Technology team. Originally from the northeast of Brazil, he has been a professional software engineer since 2007. Rafael has worked across various fields, including delivering the infrastructure behind CBS's Super Bowl LV and all Netflix live shows since 2024. He has contributed to multiple open source projects and is passionate about sharing knowledge within the tech community.

Acknowledgments

As far back as I can remember from my childhood, books were always around me thanks to a great incentive from my parents. I can remember dreaming of writing one of my own, and that at some point I wanted to be a journalist. Years passed and I ended up studying computer science; the love for reading never went away and I got to exercise my writing through technical articles. The idea of writing a book never completely faded away but it was not something that I was actively pursuing. So it was also a surprise to me when I started to work on a blog post and noticed that maybe I had enough content to fill a book.

I want to thank my parents, Regina and Marcos, for doing everything in their power to provide me with the opportunities in life that led me here. My loving wife, Isadora, for the patience and support through countless nights and weekends dedicated to writing. And Rafael, I'm lucky to have you as my brother.

I owe much of my career as a software engineer to my friends and co-founders of Vinta Software, Felipe Farias and Flavio Juvenal, and to the whole Vinta team. I couldn't have asked for a better group to share over a decade of professional and personal growth; this book would not be possible without you. I extend my gratitude to Fernando Castor, for his mastery as a teacher and for the collaboration throughout my university years.

A special thanks to Daniel Roy Greenfield, Letícia Portella, Luciano Ramalho, and Naomi Ceder, who generously shared their invaluable experience as authors when I was preparing to publish this work, and to Apress and their team for embracing this project.

ACKNOWLEDGMENTS

Thanks to Jason Santos and Pedro Barcelar for their creative work in developing the motifs and creating the illustrations opening the chapters.

Finally, I feel blessed by the number of friends who contributed some of their time reviewing the content of this book. Starting with Rafael Carício, who I met early in my professional life and who has graciously accepted the role of technical reviewer, it's an honor to work with you on this project. And to all the people who reviewed and contributed to early versions of the manuscript, my deepest gratitude, it's a privilege to call you my friends: Amanda Savluchinske, Anderson Resende, André Ericson, Bernardo Fontes, Débora Correia, Eduardo Rocha, Eduardo Silva, Flávio Juvenal, Guilherme Carvalho, Gustavo de Carvalho, Hugo Bessa, Isadora Forte, José Carlos Menezes, Lais Varejão, Letícia Portella, Luciano Ratameiro, Luiz Felipe Sotero, Mateus Gondim, Naomi Ceder, Nicole Cysneiros, Osvaldo Santana, Rafael Aguiar, Rebeca Sarai, Renato Oliveira, Rodrigo Vieira, Silas Gomes, Tarsis Azevedo, Vanderson Mota, and Vanessa Gomes.

In loving memory of *vovó* Nitinha for the companionship and shared love for books.

Introduction

Writing software is a challenging activity. There's an uncountable number of programming languages and tools you can pick from, each with their own capabilities, peculiarities, and caveats. Picking the right one will depend on what you want to achieve; for that you might need to take into consideration things like the hardware your program needs to run on and the tooling available in that language for the specific field of application.

Assuming you already have a solid basis on programming logic, it will probably take you a few days to learn the basics of a new ecosystem and perhaps accomplish some small achievements towards your goals. If this is your job and you are working on it every day, it will take a few months for you to feel like you learned the ropes and feel comfortable with that new stack. After a couple of years working in that same stack, it's likely that you've been through some major version upgrades of the tools and had to overcome a great sort of diverse issues; technical challenges will never stop to show up but they stop being as frequent and they don't scare you as much. That is until you pick up a new project with a different stack and the cycle restarts. Sometimes in the new cycle you will pick up a completely different programming language, other times you will just be using a different framework. But even when everything is supposedly very familiar, you are still starting on a new codebase written by different people who have their own styling preferences, architecture patterns, and follow different guidelines. Software development is hard.

Simultaneously, software development doesn't happen in a vacuum. Software is written to solve problems that affect people and the process of doing it is full of real world constraints. Not only do developers need to overcome the aforementioned technical challenges, they also need to learn about the business domain of the product they will be working on. Products exist to fulfill the needs of real users. Users will have diverse expectations about how things should behave, about what is missing or broken in the product and how long they are willing to wait before bugs are fixed and new features are ready to be used. In most situations, all of these decisions will be made by a network of people working for a company. Each with a designated role, a set of goals defined by their bosses, a lot of personal opinions, and motivated by their own career and financial objectives. To make things even more complex, these people need to somehow communicate and even collaborate in order to get anything done. All of that happens in the context of a market where often dozens of other similar companies are competing to see who has the best product, the most features, who can build new things faster, who is charging the least and which might be flooded with investors' money at one time and completely dry a couple months later. Again, software development is hard.

In this chaotic context, how can developers tame down the technical complexity of writing code and the chaos of a real-world business? How could one be more effective in their job? Is there a way to work that enables better results? These are complex questions but there's an interesting debate on whether software developers should be called "engineers" that can help answer them. Ultimately, I think this debate is just about a naming convention so it doesn't really matter whether or not the term "engineer" fits what we developers do. But I like to think about it as a thought exercise: if there was to be a difference between a software developer and software engineer, what would that be? When I think about "engineering" professions versus other professions, one of the things that stands out to me is how there's a constant strive for standardization. Engineers are specialists in applying scientific knowledge to the real world in a way that is efficient, safe, and repeatable. To do that, they leverage the use of tools, processes, standards, and conventions that, when properly exercised, yield consistent results. Following that logic I like to think that while both software developers and software engineers make a living through writing code, what differentiates software engineers is that they leverage tools, processes, and conventions to do their work in a more consistent way. I believe that consistency is a major differentiator because software development, as a relatively new industry, still lacks some maturity in this area and because it's an extremely valuable competence for the businesses and users we serve. To me, **the answer to the question on how we tame down the complexity of our profession and become more effective developers is by becoming better engineers, in other words, by making our work more consistent**.

In an organization, the main way to improve the delivery consistency of software teams is by adopting tools and enforcing practices that lead to better overall performance. This includes things like adopting continuous integration/delivery (CI/CD) practices, promoting the use of feature toggles or investing in monitoring tools. The existence of these tools and techniques is actually good sign that our industry is becoming more mature and all software teams should embrace them as they become the industry standard. become the industry standard Zooming down a bit, individuals can also improve the consistency of their deliveries by changing how they approach day-to-day work activities. The main caveat is that the required skills to do that are much harder to enforce from a company level: they are typically learned through observation and trial and error over years of one's career.

I'm one of the co-founders of Vinta Software and for over a decade I've built, fixed, and improved software for clients in a wide set of industries. Throughout my career, I've worked as solo engineer of projects as well as leader of teams. Over and over I was the one writing the first line of code for projects, but also many times in charge of picking up ongoing products and finding my way through huge codebases in order to deliver value to our clients as soon as possible. The content in this book is the result of all of these years of deep study, hands-on practice, discussion with peers, observation, and mentorship of teammates with the objective of building a team that consistently delivers successful software products.

The goal of this book is to explore practices that are not writing code *per se* but are an integral part of the job of any software engineer working on a business project. Anyone with a reasonable amount of experience in the area knows that writing code is only a fraction of what it takes to do this job well. In fact for many of us it's not even how we spend most of our time. Just as we continuously develop our skills in programming languages, frameworks, and software architecture, we should also invest into improving our skills in other aspects of the job as they are equally important for a successful career.

Notice that you won't find here a blueprint that suddenly makes you ten times more effective. Each of the topics we will discuss in this book will actually lead you through a series of ideas and reflections about how you can make your work more impactful by changing how you approach day to day activities. Keep in mind that there's no absolute solution that works for everyone; the ideas here are an invitation for you to reflect, experiment, and adapt to your own context.

You will notice the word "strategy" (or "strategic") is extensively used throughout the book, so it's important that we talk about it a bit. Being strategic means consciously evaluating context, factoring risks, testing solutions, planning scenarios and delivering value. For that to be effective, you need to have a clear goal. If you don't know what you want to achieve, planning becomes meaningless. Being analytical is a big factor of being strategic. Mindlessly reacting to situations means that you are not consciously deciding towards the action that gives you the most chances of achieving your goal. It's key that when you do something, you do it in an intentional way. You should know what you are doing, why you are doing it, and how it's going to bring you closer to your objective, because if it's not, perhaps you should reevaluate the situation and take another path. At the same time, being strategic also means putting aside ego in favor of collective objectives, and accepting that you need to do what it takes to reach success, not what makes you look better. Know that guarantee of success doesn't exist, so thinking in statistical terms is important. You should not expect to hit the bullseye in every decision you make. Instead, you should know that your role is to put the chances in your favor but there will always be some parts of the final result that are not in your control. It doesn't matter, your role is just to keep tipping the odds to your side. And if things don't turn out the way you wanted, that's ok, you can rest assured that you did the best you could. Finally, being strategic also means leveraging the power of collective decisions and actions, respecting and having a good relationship with teammates and valuing and practicing transparency, good communication, and alignment of expectations.

I started this book by listing what I considered to be the practices that made software engineers strategic. I was thrilled to notice that everything I listed would fit into one of four neat categories, so I divided the chapters of this book according to them: *Self-Management, Technical Discipline, Risk Management,* and *Strategic Teamwork.* In the *Self-Management* chapter (Chapter 1), we will discuss tools and techniques you can use to ensure that you are working on the right thing as well as how to make sure you are properly communicating with the people around you and making your work visible. The *Technical Discipline* chapter (Chapter 2) covers practices that make the process of writing software more predictable and efficient. It includes topics on how to improve your own workflow, and how you collaborate through code with fellow engineers. Following, the *Risk Management* chapter (Chapter 3) explores ideas on how to think critically about the impacts of your actions and how to leverage risk analysis to make better decisions. Lastly, in *Strategic Teamwork* (Chapter 4), we will dive into how to potentialize your work by collaborating with teammates and by nurturing a healthy culture of collective growth. Many of the topics we will cover are frequently associated with the capabilities expected from senior software engineers. As you climb the career ladder, you will notice that skills beyond programming, such as ownership and communication, are either required or become ever more important.

In this book you will find topics that are rarely taught to software engineers or even explicitly discussed in work environments or conferences. These are practices and skills that are often learned through observation and trial and error throughout a career in software development. Some people will have the privilege of working in teams with a strong engineering culture or have access to a versed mentor willing to help them and thus accelerating their learning curve, but most will either never pick up on some of these lessons or it will take many years of career experience until it naturally clicks for them. Here you will learn how being strategic and intentional in all of your day to day activities can make you a better engineer and propel your career.

You will be able to communicate more effectively with teammates, your leadership team, and other project stakeholders. You will learn how to make meetings more productive so you have more time to focus on your development work. You will also learn the processes and techniques that some of the most accomplished engineers use in order to deliver great code that solves problems consistently and how to collaborate with your teammates while writing software. You will notice how risk management should be an integral part of your job and the importance of actively leveraging teamwork to drive business and your own career success. So without further ado, let's start learning how to be a strategic software engineer!

CHAPTER 1

Self-Management

Self-management is undoubtedly the most important skill an engineer needs to develop in order to deliver good work over time and have it recognized by their managers and peers. That is for the simple fact that it doesn't matter how good you are at anything, if you cannot do it

© Filipe Ximenes 2024
F. Ximenes, *Strategic Software Engineering*, https://doi.org/10.1007/979-8-8688-0995-8_1

consistently over and over again, people won't trust you to do it. Being consistent is a trait that requires tweaks in many aspects of your work but that will ultimately enable you to achieve your career goals faster. By having a clear view of what are your personal goals and the business goals of your project, you will be able to actively plan the strategy that will lead you to success. Self-management skills enable all of this with the added benefit of making your work more enjoyable and allowing you to do more with less effort while being perceived as a high performer.

Engineers with low self-management skills require frequent guidance from their leadership to check up on their work and ensure things are going according to the plan. Being consistent doesn't mean never failing or always knowing what to do; you will still need guidance from time to time, but you should preemptively seek help when it's appropriate, relieving your leadership from the need of periodically checking up on you. This means that to be fully effective, self-management needs to be tackled from two perspectives: the first is actually improving the quality and consistency of your work, and the second is making sure your skills are noticed by your teammates. You need to be good at self-management and also show that you are good at it so people can trust you with the job; this applies to both your managers and your peers. Self-management is also about making it easier for your leaders to manage you as they need information about your work in order to make decisions. Provide visibility when things are looking bad but also when they are good. Reporting problems helps managers to intervene and help getting things back on track. But signaling that things are going according to the plan is also important information for them to do their work. Remember that in both situations, you should be the one who's proactively providing the visibility they need.

1.1 Keep Track of Your Activities

The number one thing in self-management is knowing what is on your plate. Make sure you know who you are responding to and frequently align expectations. Review the tools your team uses to manage activities, pay attention during team meetings and actively communicate with stakeholders. Don't start working on something or leave a meeting before you are absolutely sure about what is expected from you.

During meetings, one technique I find very effective is to always sum up and repeat out loud what you understood from it and outline top priorities. Never leave a meeting before you get confirmation that you got things right. Another powerful habit is to take notes. Writing full sentences while paying attention to what is being said is not easy for everyone, so you can practice by writing a few keywords and filling in the gaps after the meeting. For meetings that are specially important, it might be a good idea to have another person join in to be in charge of the notes. Or if it's possible use some AI tool to transcribe and sum up the conversation. Even better if you can record the meeting to watch it later. Notes are a great tool for reviewing decisions and also for ensuring no follow-up activities are missed. You can keep them to yourself or, even better, you can share them with the participants of the meeting and other stakeholders. That way they can be used as a validation step to ensure everyone is on the same page about what was decided.

Having a task management tool, such as a to-do list, to keep track of your own work-related activities is also very important. Most of your activities should be tracked and visible for the whole team in a physical or virtual board, but there will always be things that only concern yourself and that you don't want to share with everyone. This type of activity needs to be tracked somewhere and there are an unlimited number of tools that can help you with this. Try some of them and choose the one that you feel most comfortable with. A physical notepad or a simple notes application can be enough for some people. Add everything that you need to do there; even small things, if they need to be done and you are not going to do them immediately, they should be tracked. There are two goals with such an approach: (1) you should never trust your memory; and (2) you should ease your brain from the consuming task of keeping track of things to let it fully focus on the activity you are currently doing. Your personal task management tool can also be used in situations where you want to organize your ideas and plan your work in a more private environment. You can use it, for example, to break down large tasks into smaller and more manageable ones. Just be mindful that it's generaly better to keep your work public to the team. We will talk more about visibility in the upcoming sections.

It's important that you frequently review your list of activities and reprioritize it. Once you have full visibility of what you need to do, know how far are deadlines, and what is the level of importance of each task, it will be much easier to decide what is the next activity you are going to work on. Keep in mind that you don't need to blindly follow activities by their order of priority. There are other factors that you should take into account, such as size, and even your mood and energy on that day. Find a balance between these, use the moments when you are feeling most energized to start big tasks or the ones that require more creativity. When you are feeling tired, perhaps you should avoid starting new things, but you can pick something that is more repetitive or operational. Or maybe, when you only have a few minutes in between meetings, you can use that time to tackle a few of those very short ones. As long as you are frequently reassessing priorities and ensuring you are not missing any deadlines you should be fine.

Keeping your Work In Progress (WIP) low is another practice that can make you feel less overwhelmed and help you to better manage your work. It consists in having a hard limit on the amount of tasks that you've started but not yet finished, not allowing yourself to start new activities until you have completed others that are still in progress. Context switching is a big productivity killer and can lead to losing track of important activities and deadlines, reduce the quality of your work, and increase the chances of you making a mistake. WIP is also bad from the point of view of delivering value; these are activities that you've invested time on but that are not yet benefiting anyone. The sooner you finish them, the sooner your team and your customers will be impacted. Anything "done" is infinite times better than anything "in progress," as one delivers some value and the other delivers zero. If you find yourself in a situation where you have a big pile of WIP it's usually a good idea to block any new activities and spend some time just finishing the ones you've aready started until you are back to a manageable situation. As the Agile mantra by David J Anderson, creator of the Kanban, says: "Stop starting, start finishing."

And if we are talking about not missing track of work, email and notifications are certainly a major topic. One of the worst things that can happen in a professional context is your leadership and team losing the confidence that you are capable of keeping up with messages and the updates related to your activities. When this happens the natural fallout is micromanaging. **Micromanaging is an unproductive and frustrating process for everyone, even to your managers, as they will need to invest more time double-checking things, talking to you and reviewing your work.**

The main job of a leader is ensuring their team is delivering consistently despite the roadblocks and occasional individual issues. If it was easy to build perfectly self-manageable teams, there would be very little demand for them. If your manager feels that the only way to ensure your work is done is by micromanaging you, that's what they are going to do. Keep in mind that this is a pattern that is not easy to reverse, as rebuilding trust usually takes some time of intentional effort before managers feel that it's safe to step back to a healthier relationship. The best approach is always to never let yourself fall into this kind of situation.

There are whole books and uncountable blog posts describing frameworks to help you to get organized and manage your work activities. Most of them share the same basic principles: keeping your email inbox clean and using to-do lists. What works for me is adding everything to my personal to-do list, where I can periodically review and prioritize things, and using a zero-inbox technique in combination with email folders and automatic sorting filters. There's really no silver bullet here, you will need to try things out and find what best fits your personality and work routine.

Key takeaways:

- Take notes during meetings and share them with stakeholders to ensure alignment.

- Don't rely only on your memory, make extensive use of note taking and task management tools.

- Keep WIP low by focusing on finishing things before starting new activities.

- Find a process to ensure you don't miss out on notifications.

1.2 Know the Priorities

Despite requiring a wide set of skills and expectations to attend, engineers should always know what is the set of activities that are absolutely essential for their work to be considered successful. Being an engineer is a constant juggle between programming, collaborating with team members, assessing risk, and aligning expectations. Time is limited and will never be enough to do everything you want or even to do things in the way you want so knowing what the people that will be evaluating your work expect from you is essential. Having a clear view of what the main goals are will allow you to decide what to prioritize, what concessions you will make and what will need to be dropped when things don't go according to the plan. Leaders are responsible for setting up high level goals for the team, but they will not be constantly on your side helping you to make the hundreds of micro-decisions on your day-to-day activities. If you don't know what the priorities are, it's very likely that you will end up making bad decisions.

Just knowing what the priorities are is not enough, you need to understand business goals and expectations, and the constraints related to the activities you will be working on. It's inevitable that as you work you will identify unpredicted business and technical roadblocks, sometimes these will become hard blockers and you will need to consult with other people before you decide how to proceed. Other times, these issues won't be a hard requirement, but are still very important for the long-term success of the project, such as refactoring code, making improvements to an architecture, or fixing small bugs. By knowing the constraints and expectations about the thing you are working on, you will be able to make decisions about concessions you can make and how to prioritize obstacles you find in your way.

Time is perhaps the one constraint that always needs to be considered in all situations. Estimations are hard to make and they are usually wrong, so when working on something where time is a hard constraint it's better to start from what directly adds value to the product. Avoid the temptation of starting with the "side" work, finish what is essential and only then move on to the [important but] non-vital things. For instance, consider how stakeholders will feel in case they find out that a customer is still blocked because you prioritized a refactoring instead of changing the piece of code that fixes a critical bug. Not only will you be risking failing at your job but you are also risking people around you to stop trusting your judgment. **Your leadership must trust that you are able to make good decisions on your own, strategic engineers understand what success means to their stakeholders and always do it first.**

Keep in mind that leaders will not always explicitly say what they expect, as in "I want you to do X." Sometimes things will be communicated in more subtle ways such as the frequency of how they are being brought to attention, even if in a light way. If you notice that this is happening and you are not 100% sure about how important the issue is or you are not confident on how to prioritize it within your activities, ask for explicit guidance and align expectations.

If you ask your managers what their priorities are, most of the time they will be thinking about product deliveries because the success of their job depends on achieving business goals. Although knowing about these business priorities is important for you to do your job more effectively, it doesn't mean these are absolute and cannot be changed. As engineers we are the guardians of the codebase and we are the ones who understand about technical risks of the software we are writing. It's essential that we are vocal as to help managers to prioritize the things we judge as necessary for the long-term success of the software. When doing this, keep in mind that your role is to present the facts and clearly alert about the risks in a way that is accessible to the level of technical knowledge of your audience. That way they will be able to use it to decide how it compares against all the other things they have in the backlog and make an informed decision.

Teams can also have a set of policies on how they expect code to be written and managed that needs to be taken into account in your technical decisions. It's important that you know what practices and patterns are non-negotiable to your team and company. These will vastly vary depending on team size, goals, quarter, who are the stakeholders, and type of project. It's your job to learn what the policies and non-written agreements are and to adapt accordingly. For example, in some teams writing tests is non-negotiable, others teams are more flexible and might encourage engineers to judge how much of it is needed depending on the feature being developed. How much technical debt is acceptable is one of those things that will often flex depending on business constraints; in times of high pressure, it will be ok to buy debt that will be paid later on when things are less busy (we will talk more about technical debt in the *Risk Management* chapter). Clearly defining these technical policies and team agreements and getting everyone on board with them is very important to keep expectations aligned. One way to achieve this is by defining and publishing *engineering principles*. These are a set of philosophical and practical rules that will guide people to make decisions on their day-to-day job. Although technical leaders can define the engineering principles, they will work more efficiently if they are set collaboratively with everyone. Once your team decides what the principles are, publish them somewhere that is easy to find and keep referring to this document so people remember about it and review it frequently. It's also a good practice to have your own personal principles and abide by them as much as possible while following the team and company policies.

Be aware that leaders will have different expectations for different people in the team. Do not assume you just need to do whatever everyone else is doing. **Explicitly ask your leadership about what they need from you, what should be your priorities and how they would like you to report and give visibility about your work to stakeholders and to the team.** Understand what are the goals your leadership has for the team and act as a promoter of these objectives. Learn the main deficiencies that need to be addressed, what the upcoming milestones are, the business goals and even what are the expectations for other team members. Do not just wait for someone to tell you this; actively seek information and use it to help others to be successful in their jobs.

Key takeaways:

- First deliver what adds value to users and stakeholders then move to the non-critical things.

- Pay attention to what your leadership is saying and how they are saying it to identify what are the priorities.

- Be vocal to your leaders about risks and improvements that you consider important.

- Learn what are the technical policies and team agreements for writing code.

- Seek explicit orientation about what your leaders expect from you.

1.3 Make Your Work Visible

Showing the things you do, and especially the results of what you've done, is as important as doing it. Visibility is not to be confused with toxic self-promotion, these are actually opposite concepts. While toxic self-promotion is egocentric, targeting growth of individuals to the detriment of the group, visibility is all about promoting collective success, sharing risks and improving collaboration. Of course, by giving visibility you are also going to be positioning yourself to be recognized by your team members, which is certainly something that contributes to a career progression. Although in most situations this should not be your main goal, it's certainly an important aspect of visibility.

There are many positive aspects of visibility; let's start from the collaboration point of view. Developing software is a collaborative process, even when you are working alone you still need to collaborate with the users of the software in order to know what to build. Usually engineers working in a company will be collaborating with a multitude of stakeholders that are represented in many different roles such as users of the product, teammates, designers, technical leaders, business leaders, integration partners, sales, marketing people, and so on. Being a stakeholder means that these people are interested in the success of your work; either they are waiting to use the software you are developing or their own jobs depend on you delivering yours. **By giving visibility of your work you are allowing all these people to give input about it, and they will often help you to see things from other perspectives and provide valuable insights.** For instance, business people can inform you about missing functionality and possible issues with your solution as they will usually have a good understanding about the market and how users will be interacting with the product. Similarly, your teammates can provide insights on better solutions to the problem you are tackling, inform you about risks, identify performance improvement opportunities, suggest tools that can help with the task, and give tips on code reuse, quality assurance, and automated testing.

Visibility is not just about you presenting your work, all interactions you have with people at work are opportunities to provide visibility about your skills and for you to gain visibility about other people's work and how they can help you. Let's say someone asks a technical question in the team messaging app, by responding to it or participating in the discussion, you are not only helping a teammate but also showing the team that you know about that particular subject. The next time someone has a question on that topic they will know that you might have a relevant input to bring to the discussion. Actively participating in team meetings is also a great opportunity for that same reason.

Catching problems early on is one of the main goals of making your work visible as it's extremely unproductive and frustrating to invest time into something that turns out to be wrong. By frequently correcting courses and not letting things drift away too far from the path, you are increasing your chances of success by a lot. One big challenge for many people is overcoming the fear of sharing unfinished work. Drafts are a great way to validate your work with stakeholders. Make it your goal to have a simplified initial version that you can send to people and collect feedback early on. For code you can do a proof of concept, jot down your ideas in a non-working script, mock things that can be done later and even write pseudo-code. Once you get confirmation from your stakeholders that things seem to be in the right shape you can move on and invest more time on an actual version zero (and share it again). If you prefer, this can be done in a gradual fashion; for example, suppose you were asked to write a report. Start by sharing an early version with a colleague you trust and build on their feedback, then share it with your team and improve things a bit more before finally sending it to your leadership.

A less trivial question is *when* to give visibility of your work. **Sharing too much might indicate that you are insecure and have low autonomy, too little and people can lose trust because they don't know what you are doing.** There's no one right answer to this question, you will need to experiment and see what works in your context. An easy starting point is

11

to ask stakeholders how often they want to be notified about progress. You can set a time-based goal such as sending updates once a week, or you can pace reports based on achieving milestones. If you are doing the milestone approach, make sure your checkpoints are based on small achievable deliverables, otherwise you are likely to fall into a low visibility pattern. Being extra careful in situations where you get blocked is also important and these are usually a good reason for increasing the frequency of reports so other people can help to unblock you.

Communicating risks is one of the most important ways to exercise visibility. The earlier your team and stakeholders know about what can potentially break, the more time everyone has to act upon it. Be conscious about the way you are going to communicate, especially in critical situations. It's important to convey emotion in your message so people clearly perceive the gravity and intensity of the problem. A bland statement in the team message app with little context or that doesn't highlight implications will not get anyone's attention. Be specific about what is happening and the consequences of not acting on it. Saying "*feature X is critical to our checkout flow and we didn't run performance tests on it yet, I believe that this should be a high priority before we launch it live*" is much more effective than "*we haven't run performance tests on feature X.*" Also don't be afraid of being repetitive if you think something is critical. Keep pointing it out until you get an explicit answer from stakeholders acknowledging they understand it. Some risks are hard to communicate and people might not fully comprehend the first time you talk about it. Try providing details, explaining in a different way, and giving examples to catch people's attention and ensure the message is clear.

When presenting your accomplishments, the value added to the product is what everyone wants to hear from you, especially your managers. **When reporting to your leadership, make sure to prioritize showing the impact of your work to the product and to users over the process you used to achieve it.** Invest time collecting data and metrics that showcase the improvements you made and how it made the product better and users happier. If you can link your contributions to an increase in revenue it's even better. Focus on what has improved, provide metrics, show numbers and charts. Using qualitative data is ok when it's not possible to measure things objectively. Interview people to get their impressions, collect feedback, run a survey with open-ended questions. People in higher hierarchical positions are pressed to show the business outcome of the team they are in charge of, by showing the business impact of your work you are helping them to be successful and [in functional companies] that usually pays off for yourself as well.

As previously said, career growth is not the direct objective of visibility, but it's certainly a nice side effect. By practicing visibility you are reducing risks, increasing the chances of working on the right thing, and aggregating value to the business. You are also going to be perceived as a trustworthy and reliable professional by your leadership and peers.

Key takeaways:

- Collaborate with stakeholders and allow people to provide input to your work.

- Participate in team discussions to display how you can help others and learn how teammates can help you.

- Nurture the habit of sharing unfinished work so you can collect feedback and fix issues before they drift too far apart.

- Be explicit about possible consequences and risks you identify and get acknowledgement from stakeholders.

- When presenting your deliveries, focus on the value added to the business and to the product.

1.4 Ask for Help

Knowing how and when to ask for help is a trait that all engineers should learn early on. There's no point in someone's career where they are exempt from making mistakes or getting blocked. Software is written by humans so they are prone to our subjective decisions and interpretations. Variable names can be deceiving, API contracts can be broken, language paradigms have different approaches to achieve similar results and engineers are often making incorrect assumptions about the code they read and write. Even computers that are supposed to be perfectly mathematical and precise can fail due to hardware issues. Keeping a humble attitude and knowing when it's time to ask for help can save you from getting frustrated and wasting time and money.

There are many ways to ask for help and each has some kind of cost coupled to it, that cost is what you are going to balance in order to determine when to use each approach. Doing Internet research and prompting a Large Language Model (LLM) is quick, involves no one other than yourself and it will frequently get you the information you need; because of that, it should always be everyone's first choice. Try different terms in your query, do not give up on the first page of results, sometimes it's worth looking a little beyond. Internet search engines are extremely efficient, but you can get even more precision if you learn advanced features such as how to look for exact expressions, requiring or excluding terms, and filtering results from specific sites. Tweaking your LLM prompts can also be useful, use the terms you learn from answers to expand your vocabulary and improve how you ask for what you need. Another approach that is often downplayed is just reading the codebase. People get so spoiled by finding solutions online that they don't consider looking within their own project for similar solutions. Most don't invest nearly enough time carefully reading from start to end the flow of the program or digging into how things work internally. That kind of solo investigation both online and within the project codebase is very important, do not give up too early on it. Even if you don't find the solution, you'll learn a lot from it. Don't just glance at search results, pick the ones with the most potential and read them through, you will often learn something new or find insights that will help you in the future. There's no rule on how long you should try things alone, but as a reference you shouldn't give up before trying for at least ten minutes, and perhaps one to two hours is the upper limit, depending on how you are progressing.

If searching online and prompting an LLM doesn't work, the next best approach will usually be to reach for your team. Asking for help from teammates might feel like a burden because you feel that you are disturbing someone or even worse, you might feel that you are exposing yourself as being a bad engineer who couldn't solve issues by yourself. If you are constantly asking questions that you could've easily found answers to on the Internet or within project codebase and docs then yes, you are probably not acting strategically and teammates might not feel too happy. But as long as you've done a good job researching alone first, I can assure you that in most situations there's no reason for you or others to feel this way. There are many approaches to asking for help within teammates, you can send messages, schedule meetings or invite people to do pair programming with you. My recommendation is that you first try to find answers asynchronously, if that doesn't work or if it takes too long for people to respond, you then move on to more synchronous methods. It's usually better to use a public channel than a direct message, by doing that you are increasing the chances of finding someone available and getting an answer faster. When you send direct messages there's a high risk of that particular person being busy and therefore taking longer to respond. Public questions also have the benefit of allowing other people to learn from it. In all situations remember to include in your questions what you've learned so far in your own investigations. That saves you time and helps improving the quality of answers.

If reaching for your team did not help you achieve what you wanted, your next options probably are: keep trying things out, change your approach to the problem, or drop the feature. Regardless of your decision, it's going to impact stakeholders so you need to align expectations. Send a message or schedule a meeting to provide context and confirm everyone is on board with the decision.

If the decision is to keep working on the issue, there's a high chance you are now entering the dangerous realm of low previsibility work. It's nearly impossible to estimate how long it will take until you find a solution. To overcome this limitation and reduce risk, you will need to align expectations with stakeholders and start being very intentional with the frequency and quality of your reports. The worst thing that could happen is you keep working for a long time without giving visibility of progress or reassessing the situation.

If possible, this is probably the time to open a ticket either in a public forum or with the provider of the tool you are using and wait to see if someone answers with a solution or a way to circumvent the problem. For most things it's worth trying to ask a question on Stackoverflow; if it's related to an open source project, you should look for communities where you can chat with contributors and other users of the tool or open a ticket on project the issue tracker. For closed source and commercial tools, find their support channels and get in contact. But it's important to set your expectations accordingly; there's a good chance it will take a long time to get an answer and it's also possible that it will never happen, so don't sit and wait; keep searching and trying other ideas.

Another possibility is to evaluate other solutions to the problem. **Your job is to deliver value to users, not to deliver features. Think about other ways you can provide a similar value using a different solution. Brainstorm with product and design people how you could change the feature to make it simpler to implement.** Are there parts of it that could be removed with low impact to the final results? Senior engineers are constantly balancing cost and benefit to make their decisions. Almost anything can be built, the question is whether there's enough budget (or time) available.

The last option to consider is the possibility of reevaluating the feature you are working on. Just like you, project managers are constantly balancing cost and benefit to decide what gets built. It's often the case where something is sent to development just because it looks easy to do but has a limited value to the product. Bring your concerns to the stakeholders and let them decide how to prioritize that project within the new constraints against all the other projects in their backlog, it might just not be worth it to keep investing time on it right now. By sharing risks early and often, you're creating opportunities for collaboration and increasing chances of success for the team.

Remember to adapt your help-seeking strategy according to the criticality of what you are working on. Shorten the iteration loop for high risk and urgent projects: report earlier and more often, ask for more feedback, involve teammates earlier and seek external help as soon as possible.

Key takeaways:

- It's important to try things by yourself before you seek help from other people.

- Don't be afraid to ask for help, try asking questions on async channels (such as the team chat) and escalate to sync channels (such as calling a meeting) if things keep failing.

- If nothing works, escalate the situation to stakeholders so you can look for different approaches to the problem.

- The longer it takes to solve the problem the more visibility you need to give about it.

- Managers are always balancing priorities, keep in mind that in certain situations dropping or postponing the feature might be the best thing to do.

17

1.5 Get Used to Saying No

For many people, saying no feels like failing, but there are many reasons why it shouldn't be like that. In a professional environment, saying no is as good as saying yes, and often it's also more productive. Strategic engineers excel on prioritizing their work and aligning expectations, the only way for this to be done in a sustainable way is by learning to say yes and no to the right things. It's surely possible to take a large amount of work and sacrifice other aspects of your life in order to accomplish it, and sometimes that even makes sense. But you should be aiming for the long run with your career and for that to work you will need to learn how much load is reasonable to maintain that will not lead to a burnout.

The first thing we need to get over with is the idea that "superheroes," people that take on a huge amount of work, are the best employees. Superheroes are actually a liability. While trying to take on multiple parallel projects or tasks they are introducing risk to the business. Superheroes generate unreasonable expectations that ripple through the organization and lead to misalignment. They become a single point of failure as leadership will make plans counting on their promises that are constantly on the edge of failing. They assume they will never have a setback and by doing so don't plan for the unexpected. And to makes things even worse, they are often so focused on going fast that they don't bother sharing their work or their knowledge with the rest of the team. All of this generates an environment of low reliability and makes business planning much harder. The said superheroes are often professionals with poor risk management skills.

Your leaders do not expect you to always say yes. They will set expectations and ask you to do things, that's their job, but what not everyone realizes is that asking doesn't mean that they are always expecting a positive response. Leaders' job is to plan the work and promote alignment among the people they are leading. Gathering input from the team is essential for good planning, the sooner leaders know about what is the status of activities, the faster they can adapt their plans and realign expectations with customers or upper level leadership. That applies for good but especially for the bad news, as those are the ones which will cause conflict and misalignment. In functional organizations, leaders will be happy when you say no because that means you are mindful about the success of your work and that you are being honest.

Saying no is also about providing visibility and managing expectations. A project fails when it does not meet expectations, and expectations are not a rule of nature, they are social constructs humans build when interacting with each other. When you take on a new assignment from your manager you are telling them that they can expect you to get it done and therefore you will now be accountable if the results don't meet expectations. By saying no you create an opportunity for reprioritization, adaptations to the scope of projects, and better alignment. You are providing new information to stakeholders that will allow them to rethink their planning and adjust accordingly. It also allows them to move on with the orginal plan. But knowing that there's a higher risk of failure they can adjust expectations and put in place risk mitigation strategies. **Previsibility is one of the most powerful tools for a leader, by saying no you are making yourself easier to be managed.**

Keep in mind that when you say yes to something you are automatically saying no to other things, whether you are aware of it or not. For instance, when you say yes to speeding up the delivery of a feature to meet a deadline you are automatically saying no to things like carefully testing it, or dealing with edge cases. When you take a new assignment before you finish the one you are working on, you are saying no to full focus on the current activity. There's always a trade-off, it's better when we acknowledge this and make conscious decisions knowing what their consequences are.

Another downside of always saying yes and taking on too many simultaneous activities is the cognitive cost of context switching. Every time you switch the task you are working on, it takes some time for your brain to adjust to the new context before it's fully immersed and productive. **There's a performance tax to changing context and because of that it can lead to an overall performance loss.** Balancing multiple assignments simultaneously is difficult and often draining. Not only will you take longer to complete things, you will also do so by getting much more tired and stressed. Before saying yes to a new activity, make sure to factor in the downsides of context switching, often it will be better to negotiate finishing your current work before starting the new one. Even agreeing on completely pausing the current task and only getting back to it after finishing the new proposed activity will often be more effective than trying to parallelize things.

One of the reasons why saying no is hard, even if you know about the benefits and the rationale behind it, is because people perceive it as confrontation practice and not a collaborative one. For sure confronting a leader on the spot is hard. So you first need to rewire how you perceive these situations and start thinking about them as collaboration opportunities. The first thing to understand is that we are not talking about literally just saying no and walking away. Saying no is about being realistic about the work you can take on and expressing this so it can be discussed and negotiated. One thing that can help you to practice is knowing that it's often ok not to give an answer right away. When your leader asks you to do something and you are not sure how to respond or afraid of saying no, it's ok to say that you would like to think about it before answering. Ask if it's ok to get back with an answer later and take your time to evaluate the situation without the pressure of the moment. Some people don't do this because they think not having an answer right away is a sign of incompetence, but it's actually the opposite. When you do this you are indirectly telling your interlocutor that you take their request seriously and that your answer will be given after thoughtful consideration of the topic. Without rushing you can now evaluate your activities and prepare arguments before forming an opinion. When communicating back, do provide all that context along with your decision. Make it clear what are the constraints and why you think it's better to go one way or another. For negative answers, it's even better if you can propose other paths. Say things like: "I don't think we can do that in the current setup, but if we reduce the scope of X activity or join forces with the Y team there's a chance we can achieve it." Don't be afraid to renegotiate your priorities, you and your manager are in the same team, you both are shooting for the same objectives. Success is collective, either the whole team succeeds or everyone fails.

When negotiating your activities, try to focus on discussing priorities and not the amount of work. Estimates are usually imprecise and prone to big miscalculations; avoid trying to predict how much time it will take to do things and focus on getting a clear alignment on what needs to be done sooner. If you know what the goals are you will be able to prioritize your work and propose an adequate plan, saying yes to what matters and saying no to everything else.

Key takeaways:

- Your leaders expect that you say no to the things that don't look viable because that's valuable information for planning.

- Time is limited, when you say yes to something you are implicitly saying no to other things.

- Context switching is a productivity killer, saying no allows you to focus on what matters.

- Saying no creates opportunities for collaboration and reprioritization.

1.6 Problem-Solving Mindset

Every project is loaded with problems; no engineer in the works in a place where they can confidently say that everything is perfect, there's no technical debt, no pressure from stakeholders, all team members are satisfied with their work and growth and all users are happy. If you know someone that feels like that it's probably because they are working full time alone on a personal project that will never be outed to other people. Their product probably also doesn't integrate with any other software and is absolutely non critical. Managing and solving problems is the very nature of software engineering; internalize this and focus on what you can control: prioritizing and getting things done.

As you work on a codebase it's natural that you identify bugs, code quality issues, performance bottlenecks, and refactoring opportunities. It's expected that all engineers report about these problems so they can be prioritized and addressed before they become a risk. But, strategic engineers go one step further, they report issues alongside solution proposals. **Just shedding light on the things that need to be addressed is already a great practice and an important contribution to any team, but kicking off discussions from an initial proposal that can be built upon is a lot more productive and effective.** Proposing a solution requires effort as you will need to do some investigation to understand context and constraints before settling on an idea and you want to be mindful about how you spend your time. If it's not a critical thing or a low priority issue, then limit your investigation to a proportionally reasonable time; it's not wise to lose focus on your main activities just to propose a solution to something that is not that important. If you are not sure about the priority, take it to your leadership, ask for confirmation and for more context before digging deeper and investing more time.

After you've identified a problem that you'd like to fix and planned a possible solution to it, you still need to get your team on board before actually starting working on it. Find an appropriate moment to share your ideas with them and get a feel on how people relate to the matter. Explain the problem you've identified and how it affects you and other people in the team, show your proposed solution, highlight the benefits, the risks, and collect feedback on it. By getting other people to support and promote your ideas you are increasing the chances of getting a buy-in from your leadership to work on it.

Proposing solutions is also about taking work from people instead of adding. Leaders are busy people, they have a lot on their plate and are constantly context switching and rethinking priorities in order to respond to stakeholders needs. When you bring in a new issue without assessing it or proposing a solution, it feels like you are just adding more to their plate. Unless the problem you are bringing to attention is clearly a priority, it's very unlikely that your leader will stop what they are doing to do this investigative work. A way to reduce that kind of noise is by addressing low-hanging fruits right away instead of bringing them to discussion. Strategic engineers can play a key role in solving problems that improve the team's performance and quality of life as this kind of work is often very strategic but hard to be prioritized by managers. By getting these out of the way without the need for it to go through the full cycle of prioritization, you are reducing cognitive load and speeding up the process. Career wise, the more you are perceived as a work reliever, the more valuable you will be for the team which will likely translate into promotions.

One of the worst nightmares for a manager is an engineer that is constantly complaining about problems but never proposes solutions. Managers are facilitators, they coordinate demands from multiple sources and organize the work removing blockers. They usually are aware that there are an uncountable number of problems in the product and their job is to balance stakeholders expectations and solve one problem at a time. Having someone expecting problems to magically get solved is frustrating. Notice that the key here is *form*; complaining is different from reporting, the way you communicate is what is going to determine if your message will be perceived as one or the other. Complaints are usually poorly structured, they don't consider context and they don't propose ways forward. So it feels like the goal is just to dump problems in other people's hands, not to collectively build toward a shared goal. Reports, on the other hand, are constructive; they are about providing visibility and improving things for everyone. Practice complaining less and reporting more.

In certain situations it's ok to complain, sharing work-related frustrations and anxieties can be a great way of relieving yourself. You are not a robot, your feelings matter and in a functional work environment sharing them should be encouraged. But if you are going to do so, do it during one-on-one meetings, preferably with your leadership. Dumping unstructured or unactionable problems in front of the whole team leads to very unproductive discussions that lower people's morale and has no benefit for you or anyone. The same goes for having that kind of conversation with less experienced teammates. Junior engineers normally won't have the maturity to deal with the situation, they will absorb things and be negatively influenced. There's also a high risk that they will become boosters of your frustrations which can contaminate other people and lead again to lowering the team morale. If you need to complain, do it directly to your leaders, they are the ones that should know how to deal with it. They can help you structuring your thoughts and have the power and the tools to address the issue in the best way possible.

Beware of the kind of problems you are taking to your leaders, they are there to help with work-related issues. We all have our own personal problems and while it's ok for you to share them to provide context about why you are facing a certain situation, it's not their job to provide emotional support to you, neither do they have the necessary training to do it. Perhaps there's someone in the people department who can better assist you, or you should seek professional help outside of work.

Key takeaways:

- Shed light on the problems you identify and propose solutions as you do it.

- Be a promoter of the issues you consider important to be addressed so you can get more people on board on the cause.

- Low hanging fruits don't need to be prioritized by your manager, fix them yourself and report back as a done job.

- Be mindful about what, how, and who you complain to.

1.7 Own Your Career

Your career is yours only to manage; never delegate it to someone else because, in the end, only you know what you want for yourself. That means you should not wait for companies to tell you what you have to do in order to grow, you should proactively discover what are the next steps that will take you where you want to be. The main reason for that is that you have little control over what the company's plans for you are, and there's a reasonable chance they are not perfectly aligned to your own goals, or even worse, the company simply might not have a plan for you. Strategies for managing your career will greatly vary depending on the nature and size of the company you are working at, so experiment different approaches and find out what works best in your situation.

In order to own your career, the first thing you will need to know is what are your career goals. What do you aspire to do? How fast you want to get there should be less important but still relevant to think about. It's great to have very long-term goals, like ten years from now, these are important to serve as a north star and to keep you motivated, but it's hard to plan for such a long stretch. Instead, focus on your next one to two years. Observe teammates that are ahead of you in the career ladder and check whether your self-expectations are reasonable. It's important that you set a goal that is achievable otherwise it's likely that you will get frustrated and hinder your motivation to keep progressing.

Keep in mind that owning your career doesn't mean ignoring the career plan from your company; on the contrary, it means leveraging the tools you have available to achieve your goals, and a career plan is one of the best tools for that. So start from the basics and make sure you have visibility of the company's official career plan. If your company does not have one, ask your leadership to provide one. It doesn't need to be a super-detailed document with exact requirements for each level, especially if you work in a small company, even a more abstract document that talks about aspirations for the main levels of the ladder should be enough for you to get started. Regardless of what your career goals are, the company is the one that will decide whether you grow or not, so you need some reference to understand what they value, what they expect from you, and how you are being evaluated. Without that information it's going to be very hard to be strategic and make an effective growth plan.

The last thing you should consider before starting to work on a career plan is good visibility on the current business goals of the company. Is this publicly posted somewhere? If not, find someone that can answer that for you. Consider your team/project goals as well. Your impact is always going to be measured primarily by the people near to you so your plans need to take into account what these people are expecting from your work.

Once you have visibility of the company career plan, their current objectives, and know where you want to be in a couple years, you can then define a strategy for your career and the steps to getting to where you want to be. **Know what is your long-term goal but don't plan how you are going to get there all at once; define a practical goal that you can objectively complete and avoid things that are hard to measure or that are too subjective.** Choose something that you can achieve in a few months, planning over three to four months is a good reference. Achieving your goal within the planned time span is important for you to feel that you are progressing. For example, if you are aiming to improve your technical writing skills perhaps you could set a goal to write two or three blog posts in the upcoming quarter and have them reviewed by your peers so you can gather feedback. These periodic checkpoints will keep you motivated in order to build toward your long-term goal. The easiest way to reach far is by compounding short and frequent progress.

To make sure you have a solid strategy, write your goals in a document and share them with your direct leadership and the people that have a chair evaluating your career progression. Most engineers only talk about their career with their leadership once a year during performance reviews. This is a very risky way of managing your career as many things can go wrong along the way. For instance, company goals might change, expectations for you and your role can be updated or you might simply have misunderstood alignments from the last performance review. You should validate your plan before executing it and keep collecting feedback while it's being executed; that allows for correcting the course in case of misalignments. Schedule a meeting with your leaders and present your 3-month plan, confirm that it aligns with their expectations, confirm that it's a reasonable amount of work (not too much, not too little), get their confirmation that by achieving the goals you are going to be on the right track to receive a promotion in the next year. Every three months schedule a new meeting to show your progress with the initial plan and present the plan for the next three. If you keep aligning expectations and getting leadership's buy-in, it's going to be very hard for them to justify not promoting you.

Be explicit about your long-term career goals; by knowing where you want to be in the next few years, your leadership can provide opportunities for you to thrive. As much as you should be paving your own way, you will always be subject to the context of the project and company you are working for. Sometimes it will not be possible to align company plans with yours; if this is the case, you might have to make the decision to either find a new job or to pause or change your plans for some time. These rigid situations are not too common; in most companies, it's possible to find opportunities that directly or indirectly take you in the path you want to steer your career. Communicate your long-term goals to your leadership so they can help create opportunities and guide you when opportunities arise. For instance, if you want to be a tech lead or an engineer manager they could find opportunities for you to practice leadership skills. Or perhaps you are an experienced front-end engineer but would like to develop your backend skills and they can put you in a project that allows that. At the same time it's also important that you don't expect a huge change; your leadership will not adapt all of your attributions just because you mentioned your plans. You are still a valuable asset doing the things you are known to be good at right now. You will need to slowly start demonstrating you are capable of being productive in the areas you want to develop before your leadership is comfortable giving you more responsability in it. The other benefit of being explicit is putting yourself for consideration in case a position aligned with your plans opens up, that's especially useful if you are aiming for management roles.

Notice the main concept behind the ideas we've been discussing is to validate your plans early on so you can align expectations with your leadership. It's possible to shorten this validation loop even further by constantly asking for feedback. You don't need to wait before you've completed major milestones in your career to sync with your leadership, the faster you ask for feedback on your progress the sooner you can course correct and avoid wasting time on the wrong thing. While it's desirable that your leadership is proactively helping with your career development, you are the one responsible for making it happen, so don't wait on others, explicitly ask for feedback throughout the process.

The best ways to get recognition in a company is either by directly contributing to whatever are their current objectives or by positively impacting revenue. Notice these are different things, more money is not always a good thing. A startup strategy might be 100% focused on growth regardless of money spending. If this is the case and you decide to invest your time on optimizing infrastructure costs, you are actively going against the company strategy even though you might be saving them money. If the current strategy is growth, the best use of your time is building things that will bring more users. Keep in mind that it's virtually impossible to only be working on things that you like or that are aligned with your career objectives, so you need to learn how to align what you want with what the company needs. It's very unproductive for you and for the company if you keep pushing against their strategy just to fulfill your career goals. If you find yourself in this situation, it's probably better to just look for another place to work that is more aligned with your plans. But, considering you want to stay, do your best to understand what is the current strategy and point your goals in the same direction. Not only will it be easier for you to achieve them but you are also increasing the chances of being recognized and promoted faster. Pay attention to what c-levels and your direct leadership are saying during company meetings. These will usually be used to communicate what is the strategy and to point out what the current issues are. Notice what is being frequently brought up to attention, what topics are more often mentioned, and what is being emphasized. Communication is not always explicit, pay attention to the nuances and react fast to changes.

Another way to tip the odds slightly in your favor is to follow the money. Understand the business of your company and find which are the products and services that generate the most revenue to it and work in these projects. These areas will usually be the ones receiving more investment and are more resilient to survive periods of crisis and market downturns. It's much easier to prove the value of your work to the company when it's directly generating more money. Areas that are not core to the business are often treated as cost centers. They are still important and needed but managers will always try to squeeze the most out of them to save money. When business is not going well, these are the projects which will face budget cuts and layoffs first. Take into account the macroeconomics; is software engineering a profit or cost center in the industry you are working at? Think about this when deciding to switch jobs and comparing proposals. Companies will often assemble teams to experiment new areas of business, or to take on "innovation" projects.

Be aware when joining this kind of initiative; while they can take on and consolidate as a new profit center, the odds are usually against them, for one of those to be successful many will fail. On the other hand, if you join one of these teams and they turn out successful, as one of the early members you are going to naturally be in a privileged position. Make an informed decision considering the risks; one right shot and you can catapult your career, but consider the possibility of having a few failures before getting one right.

While your leadership should be your main reference point, you can always make use of some external help. Mentors are usually people who are more experienced or have been longer in the company than you. Because of that, they have a good understanding of the dynamics of the work environment and can pass on their learnings so you can find shortcuts and avoid the same mistakes and pitfalls. Some companies have an official mentorship program; if that's your case, don't hesitate to make good use of it. If there's no official program, you can still find someone and ask them for a few minutes per month of their time to chat about your career. Don't think you are going to be bothering them, most people will be happy to help you out. Look for people that are in career paths similar to yours and that you consider to be role models, ask your peers for references of people they think would be a good mentor. Preferably choose someone that is not working directly with you so you can benefit from an impartial external perspective. Needing to explain and provide context is going to be a good exercise for you to reflect on the topics of discussion. Don't be afraid to switch mentors, people will give advice based on their own experiences of the world and their unique process dealing with problems. It's ok if you feel that mentorship sessions are not working with someone, thank them and try with someone else until you find a person who understands your perspective and gives advice that resonates with you. Mentorship sessions should not be a status report of your work, they are a place to discuss career challenges, remove blockers, and gain perspective and motivation when you are feeling frustrated. There's not much point in having weekly mentorship sessions, but having them too far apart is probably not very useful either. The best frequency will of course depend on yours and your mentor's availability, but one to two months is probably the sweet spot. Lastly, it's important to remember that it's your job to bring an agenda for discussion, mentors are there to share their experiences but they will not plan your career for you. You should be the one proposing the topics to be discussed, prepare for the meeting in advance and be strategic; remember that someone is kindly offering their precious time to you, so you should make good use of it.

Key takeaways:

- Define clear goals for your career.

- Leverage your company's career plan.

- Know what are the short- and mid-term business goals of your team and use them in your favor.

- Write down a mid-term strategy composed of small achievable checkpoints.

- Be vocal to your leaders about your career goals and ask for feedback frequently.

- Find a mentor, ideally one that is currently in or beyond the job title you are aiming at.

1.8 Take Control of Your Time

If you were ever part of the initial team of a startup you will notice how much easier it is to work with a small team in a fresh code base. As projects mature and the team grows, everything becomes more complicated; there's more planning, more process, more documentation, and meetings – lots of meetings. Before you know, a big chunk of your time is gone on pre-scheduled activities and you start to feel very unproductive. Engineers should be strategic about their time and periodically review their calendar looking for what can be optimized. There are two principles I use for good time management, they are: reducing context switching and planning idle time.

Being intentional about the use of your time is essential; in any non-trivial work environment, just letting things run their natural course is the formula for unproductivity. From time to time, review your agenda and reorganize events. Start from the reduce context switching principle: how are meetings plotted over your week? If you aren't being strategic about meetings, they are not only consuming your time but are also consuming your mental bandwidth. It's very hard to end a meeting where you actively participated and jump straight into a focused programming session, you will need some time to cool down and rewire your brain for the new context before you are productive. With that in mind there are a few things you can do to optimize your time.

First thing is clustering meetings whenever possible. If you are attending meetings that are all over your day, try moving them to a single period, morning or afternoon; the goal is to reduce the amount of time you have to switch from meeting mode to focused mode. It's a lot more productive to have big blocks of focused, uninterrupted work. When clustering meetings, do consider a five-to-ten minute interval between them so you can go to the bathroom, drink water, and review the agenda before jumping into the next one. Avoid those 20-to-40-minute gaps that are not enough to get anything done or worth making the switch to focused mode.

Don't rule out the possibility that some meetings are not productive or just not worth your time. Check if you really should be attending all the meetings in your agenda. Propose experiments, suggest to your team replacing a certain meeting with an async discussion for a month and evaluate the results. Or make it a policy that it's not rude for people to skip meetings if they feel their participation is not needed or that they are not feeling productive. That kind of thing can also have the side effect of forcing meeting facilitators to be more strategic and intentional on how they run meetings and select the topics to be discussed. Consider proposing a no meetings day, a day of the week when it's forbidden to schedule any meetings.

At Vinta, we had a team that was having trouble meeting their goals and people were feeling unproductive and frustrated. So we set down to evaluate what was going on and identify what could change to improve the situation. Among other things, we noticed that this team had a lot of meetings, many of them requiring everyone's attendance. We decided to try a radical change, we canceled stand ups, recurring one-on-one's, and retrospective meetings, replacing them with a single short weekly meeting per squad. The results were outstanding, people started collaborating more fluidly through existing communication channels and used the weekly squad gathering just to discuss more pressing issues. The fact that there were less people in the meetings was also key as it made squads more focused on topics relevant to their particular context. Upon request from the engineers, we kept a "tech sync" meeting that was used to discuss and showcase architecture and technical topics relevant to the whole engineering team. It was still possible to have meetings with the whole team, but those were not recurrent and only called for topics that required it. Meetings should exist out of necessity to fulfill clear goals. Team dynamics, and project goals change over time, resetting the agenda helps identifying what is still relevant and getting rid of unproductive time.

Block periods of your week with two-to-four-hour slots for focused work. Make it hard for people to schedule meetings in these periods and only allow it as a last resort. The goal here is to have predictability on at least a few moments of your week that you can count on to sit down and get things that require focus. When entering focus mode, try to shield yourself from distractions, close your email tab and even your company chat app if you feel that it will help (but make sure people know how to reach you in case of an emergency). Also block time slots in your calendar for activities that you need to do recurrently, for example, if you have to send a report at the end of every week. That way you prevent people from scheduling thing in that period and ensure you will be able to focus to get things done in time. Create a healthy relationship with internal communications tools, if you get anxious with email notifications, avoid constantly checking it, reserve specific time slots to review and answer email messages. Perhaps you can do it once when you start working just after you get back from lunch. It's usually good to also check it before you leave for the day to ensure you don't miss any time-sensitive demands.

Planning for idle time is the second principle and the reason it's important is because you need to always account for the unplanned. If you are constantly taking up work that fills 100% of your time, it means that whenever there's a change in the initial plans, such as an urgency, blocker, or unplanned scope addition, it's guaranteed you are going to fail. Let's be honest, adapting to unpredicted situations is just the nature of the work of a software engineer. **Estimating is a tool for prioritization and risk management, not a way to exactly predict how long things will take to get done.** When you are planning your week, make sure it has some idle time; there's a high chance it will end up being filled by the last-minute changes and emergencies. And if for some reason it ends up as free time, that's great, use it to anticipate other activities and collaborate with teammates. By now it should be clear to you that one of the most important things in your job is to align expectations; it's always better to over-deliver than it is to fail agreements.

Be in control of your work, don't just react to whatever shows up in your day. That's what will allow you to work smart, have a good work-life balance and sustain a long and healthy career. Standing up, stretching, drinking water, and exercising regularly also helps a lot.

Key takeaways:

- There's a tax to switching from meeting mode to focused work mode; cluster meetings and avoid unproductive time gaps between them.

- Increase async collaboration and experiment with your team for ways to reduce the amount of meetings and their durations.

- Block time in your agenda for focused work.

- Ensure there's margin in your planning so the unexpected can be accommodated.

1.9 Be Strategic During Meetings

Meetings, both team and one-on-ones, are an important part of an engineer's job. When well conducted, they enable alignment and improvements of team and individual practices and processes. At the same time most people would love to have as little as possible of them as they often consume a significant amount of time, impacting productivity. The best way to achieve a balance is to make sure the time invested on them is effectively used. It's not uncommon to find engineers who despise meetings, and if this is the case for you, it's probable that either you or your team are not making good use of these collaboration moments. In this section, we are going to talk about individual practices that can make meetings more productive and hopefully even enjoyable. If after applying these techniques you still find yourself resenting these moments, it's probably a good idea to bring this up for discussion with your team and reevaluate the format or even reconsider the actual need for some of the meetings. If it's not being productive it might be better to simply cut it back.

The process of making meetings effective starts before people get together to talk; the first rule of a good meeting is having a preset agenda. There's no way to be effective if you start a meeting that doesn't have a clear goal. Having an agenda serves to align everyone's expectation on what's to be accomplished and why it's important that everyone's time is being invested on it. Make sure that whenever you invite someone or a group of people to talk there will be an agenda that is easy to find and open for everyone to see. By doing this you are going to be preparing yourself for the meeting and also allowing others to do so. The more people are prepared for the meeting the higher are the chances of it being short and productive. Meetings with a loose scope tend to last longer, be less focused, and produce low quality outcomes. Be specific with your agenda topics, and if needed, write something to give participants context or provide links they can use to review information about what's going to be discussed. And if you get invited to a meeting that doesn't have an agenda, don't be afraid to ask people to provide one. Your time is valuable and it's your job to make sure it's going to be well spent.

Once you ensure that all meetings you attend have an agenda, the next step is to use this information to prepare for the meetings. For instance, if your team is meeting to discuss the next quarter OKRs, at the very least you need to review the OKRs prior to the meeting. It will be even better if you also prepare questions and topics for discussion. Especially when meeting with leadership, review the agenda and try to think about what questions you will need to answer. Invest some time collecting the data and information to answer these questions and make sure they will be easy to access and present when you need them. Review linked documents and get acquainted with topics you might not have enough context such as a certain business domain or a part of the code you haven't worked with yet. If you're not sure what one of the topics is about, send messages to your teammates and try to collect more information. Review if you don't have questions or suggestions related to the topics that could be addressed during that time.

Remember that the only way to participate in a meeting is not just by making assertive comments, often by asking good questions you are already generating a lot of positive value to the process. The habit of preparing for meetings is not easy to develop, it requires some practice. A good way to kickstart it is forcing yourself to have ten minutes of focused time before each meeting just thinking about it. Eventually you will get used to the process and it'll happen more naturally.

Preparation is especially important for one-on-one meetings as your participation is absolutely required for the success of them. These are often one of the few opportunities you'll get the undivided attention of someone, especially from leaders who are usually on a tight schedule. For recurring sessions it's a good idea to have a shared document where both participants can input topics as they surface in their day-to-day work. Leaders need to feel confident that you understand what is being said and it's frustrating to talk to an apathetic audience. Pay attention to your body language, use nods to provide feedback and demonstrate you are attentive. Asking questions and making comments help build the sensation that there's alignment and commitment (if you want to research more about this the keywords are "active listening"). Keep in mind that disagreeing is as important as agreeing. Don't restrain from speaking your mind; by doing so you are creating opportunities for more discussion and enabling that an alignment is eventually reached. One-on-ones are also a great opportunity to make bonds with the people you work with. Use a few minutes at the beginning of the meeting to chat about non-work topics, perhaps you can share something fun you did in the weekend and make conversation with the other person. Building these relationships is strategic for your career and it's a way to do team building.

When talking in a meeting, it is important that you balance what and how much you are going to share:

- Who is your audience?

- How much detail do they need *right now*?

- How much time do you have available to talk?

- What could be better explained or debated asynchronously through text?

- What parts of the content is your audience most interested in?

- What is the main message you want to convey?

- What is the outcome you are seeking?

People's attention span is usually very low, you should be strategic and really adapt your discourse to maximize the chances of accomplishing what you want from the meeting. For broader audiences it's usually better not to dig into the details (unless that's the goal of the meeting). Give just enough context so everyone knows what you are talking about and move on to the conclusions. Be as direct and practical as possible, expect that broader audiences will not capture the nuances. Limit yourself to two or three main messages, more than that and it's likely that people will not remember everything. Consider that when you bring too much information it becomes harder for people to distinguish what are the key topics they need to take away. Be objective and explicit about what is essential, what the priorities are, and the actionables you want to highlight.

At Vinta we had a teammate who was having trouble communicating during meetings. It was hard for that person to moderate what they should be reporting, they were often too technical, beyond what the audience would find useful. Besides that, it was the first time in their career that they had to report to business people so that made them nervous, which contributed to worsening the problem. To help, we proposed doing some practice sessions before the meetings. First, the person would draft what they wanted to say and send it for revision. During this process I'd suggest resources that could help the audience understand the message, such as doing a screen share or preparing a few slides. After a few feedback rounds, once the content was better tuned we would schedule a quick session to practice the presentation. After doing that a few times, the person understood what was expected for these meetings and was able to prepare for following ones with less intervention.

Effective meetings should start with a planned agenda, have a participative audience, and end with clear and actionable items. Closing meetings with a recap of what was discussed and what the agreed next steps are is a great way to promote alignment and ensure everyone is on the same page and set for success. This is especially effective during one-on-ones with your leadership. By recapping topics before leaving, you are double-checking you fully understand instructions and adding yet another layer to prevent misalignments.

Key takeaways:

- Ensure all meetings have an agenda that is shared with all participants.

- Prepare in advance for meetings, gather the information you will need and elaborate questions.

- Be especially attentive in one-on-one meetings so you can take advantage of this focused time with your leadership.

- Adapt your discourse according to the audience and meeting goals.

- Recap decisions and action items before leaving the meeting.

1.10 Effective Text Communication

Through programming languages we communicate to computers the steps we want them to execute, but these languages go beyond that, they are also built to be understandable by humans. Good code communicates to other programmers our intentions and allows them to effectively add functionality, change behavior, and fix problems. Engineers must be good code communicators, but it is as important that they are effective through other forms of text communication such as writing code comments, documentation, tutorials, guidelines, discussions, and even the day-to-day chat messages with the team. Effective writers can quickly formulate text that is clear, informative, and short. This is no easy feat as stated by the famous Pascal quote: "The present letter is a very long one, simply because I had no leisure to make it shorter."

Poorly written text can be very harmful in the context of software engineering, it can produce misunderstandings that will ultimately lead to more bugs, incorrect or inconsistent business logic and misaligned expectations between you, your peers, and managers. In its many forms and contexts, good writing is directly related to your performance as an engineer. Developing the skill of writing effectively is a great investment in your career. The best way to do it is by practicing, so start early and don't be afraid to make mistakes – that's how you are going to learn. Be intentional in everything you write, think about the message you are trying to convey, read it out loud to confirm it's clear, check for inconsistencies, and provide all the context your audience needs to effortlessly understand your message. People are lazy so you need to make it easy for them to consume and understand what you write in order to successfully deliver your message. Highlight the main topics, provide external links, use paragraphs to group information. Our brains are bad at processing too much information at once, it will naturally try to select and focus on what it perceives as the most important thing and ignore everything else. Account for that in your writing, avoid mixing things from different contexts, don't ask too many questions all at once, and if you need to do so, provide an interface that will allow your audience to focus on one question at a time (such as a form). Until you are confident about your writing skills, ask for explicit feedback from your peers. Ask if the message was clear and if any part of the text could have been written differently in order to sound clearer and confirm they got all the context they needed. Remember, if you feel insecure with messages or documents that go to a broader audience you can send it to someone you trust for review before making it public.

As more and more companies adopt remote or hybrid work, async text communication becomes an even more important skill to software engineers. For this type of work arrangement to be effective the standard should be that if there's one person working from home everyone needs to adopt remote work practices, that's the only way to ensure the people working remotely are properly included in the team workflow. So whether you like remote work or not, chances are that you will need to develop skills that enable it, and text-based communication is one of the bases of it. For global teams, it's even more important as engineers from different countries will usually have few overlapping work hours; in this situation, writing effectively becomes a necessity in order for these teams to be productive. Other day-to-day activities that show the importance of text-based communication to all software engineers include: commenting and documenting code, doing code reviews, writing incident reports, and reporting in the team issue tracker.

Text-based communication is also about visibility; people frequently use chat-based direct messaging and one-on-one meetings to discuss things that could benefit the whole team. Using public channels for discussions is not necessarily about having everyone participating in them; one of the main benefits is actually allowing other people to gain context about what is being talked about. This is the kind of information that might not be useful immediately but that can be extremely helpful in the near future. Teams grow and people change jobs, so being able to reference past discussions and decisions is a super power that enables scaling and reduces risk. Other benefits of text-based async communication include allowing people to think and prepare before answering questions, being fast to consume, being searchable, being referenceable and enabling linking to specific parts, and being editable so it can be updated as things change.

While asynchronous communication has many benefits, synchronous communication remains crucial. Many situations, such as sensitive or time-constrained situations, are better addressed through real-time, synchronous interactions. If you have work that is blocked, you should certainly leverage your team to get back on track as soon as possible. War rooms are extremely effective for tackling critical incidents. Team ceremonies such as retrospectives also benefit from the dynamics of video conferencing or being physically in the same place as your team. But even in these situations, summing up decisions and publishing them in a written document is beneficial. The team building aspect of synchronous communication is one aspect that is hard to reproduce in async channels and that should be accounted for. As mentioned before, async and sync communications can complement each other. For instance, instead of meeting to introduce a topic, you can first publish a document to get everyone on board with the basics and use a meeting to promote discussions and answer questions, making the meeting much more productive and interesting.

As seen, there are many benefits to being an effective writer and the best way to improve on it is by practicing. It's a skill that you can develop, and as any other, it will be hard in the beginning but it will eventually become effortless and natural. Asking for feedback from your peers is often the easiest way to learn what you can do better.

Key takeaways:

- Be intentional with your writing, ensure the message is clear and the content is easy to consume.

- Prefer public channels over private messages to increase visibility and collaboration.

- Practice by asking peers to review and provide feedback about your writing.

1.11 Reporting

The job of your leaders is to ensure that their teams are consistently delivering; that is achieved through aligning expectations up and down and unblocking people. In order to do these things, they need visibility of the work being done by the team. That is, either the team self-reports or they need to be frequently asking for updates. Frequently asking for updates is very inefficient and time-consuming for all parties involved as it requires more communication and context switching, so getting better at self-reporting is an important skill for engineers. Failing to report well has similar consequences to failing to keep track of your activities and might lead to micromanaging. By learning to report effectively you are making yourself more reliable and easier to manage.

Frequency of reporting is usually the hardest part to get right because there's no rule that fits all cases. You will need to leverage priority, urgency, risk, context, your role, and the overall mood of the project in order to determine how much and when you should be reporting. Having your leadership asking you about progress of your work is probably the best reference point to determining you should've reported earlier. Keep in mind that there are downsides in over-reporting; it might indicate low maturity and insecurity from you. Although reporting too much is not ideal, it's certainly better to overdoing it than to not be doing it enough. As you experiment, ask for explicit feedback on your reporting frequency. It's a good idea to determine a fixed reporting frequency for each of your attributions. For instance, you might plan to send a message to your leadership every week communicating progress on a project that has a deadline in two months, but that will be too little for a project estimated to be done in a couple of weeks. Remember that reporting is not just about communicating the problems. Informing that things are on track and even that there are no updates is just as insightful. Having a fixed frequency goal helps setting the expectations on what is the minimum you should be reporting. Factors such as blockers, previously unknown risks, and deadlines getting closer serve as alerts to indicate you should increase your reporting frequency so you need to adapt as quickly as possible to these.

Be strategic with the content of your report, adapt the message to the audience and to the context. Consider the level of detailing and technical information you are going to provide. When you are reporting to a more technical person it might make sense to provide a lot of details as that person can unblock problems, give feedback, and provide insights on things you might not have considered. To others that kind of information might just be unproductive and noisy. The same factors that determine frequency should also be taken into account here, usually the level of detail you should provide increases as the risks go up. How you are going to report also matters; it's a good idea to call a meeting to report urgent things. For non-urgent matters it's probably a better approach to send a detailed document that can be discussed asynchronously and call a meeting in case it needs a more active collaboration on certain topics. The advantage here being that synchronous meeting time is used only to discuss the hot topics, not to introduce the matter. This approach is more efficient and considerate to everyone's time. Be propositive whenever possible, don't just say you have a problem, tell what your plan is for fixing it as well. Make it easy for people to consume your reports. Not everything needs to go in, filter what is really relevant to keep things short as possible, use bullet points and highlight the most important items. Clearly identify the risks and if there's anything you need answered. Effective reports are optimized to have a low consumption of time and headspace of the person receiving it. The success of your work is going to be directly impacted if your leadership misses important information. By facilitating things for them you are making their work more effective and in return allowing them to help you to be successful in yours.

Reporting is a topic that encompasses many of the things we previously discussed. It's all about working on the right thing, providing visibility, asking for help, and communicating (especially through text), and just like these it's also a skill you can develop through practice.

Key takeaways:

- There's always value in reporting so share good and bad news and even when there is no news.

- Learn what is the right frequency to report according to your context and the activity you are working on.

- Adapt the level of details depending on your audience, the risks, and urgency of the matter.

1.12 Keep Up with Technology

It doesn't take a lot of time working in software to understand how fast things change compared to most other areas of work. The speed in which new tools, processes, languages and frameworks get created or significantly changed can be overwhelming. Although some people build whole careers around the same technologies, this might not be the average experience. Most engineers will change their technical stack a few times over they career either because of changing jobs or because they are upgrading their toolset to more modern technologies. While the fast pace of change is certainly welcome as a great source of innovation and maturity growth for the industry, it comes with a significant burden on engineers who need constant adaptation and requalification in order to stay up-to-date with the best practices and tools. For anyone in tech, the challenge is keeping up a growth pace that is steady, fits your work and life routine, and is sustainable in the long run.

One of the hardest questions to answer on the topic of personal development is when to do it. Usually everyone is very busy with their day-to-day work and personal life issues so it's hard to manage anything that doesn't seem absolutely essential. The ideal solution to work on personal development is to build a routine by reserving some time every day to study a bit, in the same way that you should have a physical exercise routine. When done correctly, using 15 to 30 minutes per day for personal development should have no noticeable impact on your work deliveries, especially if you match what you are studying with the problems you are dealing with at work. Consider doing it at the beginning of the day which is the moment when you are not tired, messaging channels are quieter, and you don't have other activities taking up space on your brain. Young people beginning their careers usually need more time than that, but they have the advantage of being more eager to grow and have more energy to invest. Not everyone has the privilege of being able to study outside of working hours due to their personal life context, but if you can do it it's probably a good investment of your time and likely to allow you to jump levels on the career ladder a bit faster.

Picking a topic to study is especially difficult for less experienced people because either they don't know what knowledge they are missing or there's too many things to learn and it's hard to prioritize. For people in this situation it can be productive to seek a mentor or a coach to provide some guidance. Generally it's recommended that you start from the topics which are in direct demand for your job and explore others topics of interest after you are comfortable with the day-to-day ones. For more experienced engineers, what frequently happens is that they get caught up on their operational work and forget to look outside for what is new and how to improve what they have. In this case, there are two main forms of keeping up-to-date, one is to build a process that allows the new content to periodically get to you (let's call this cumulative learning) and the other is to intentionally choose topics to specialize in and build deep knowledge (let's call this specialization learning). The former helps with your day-to-day growth and generates knowledge that is usually directly applicable in your work and the latter helps with your long-term career development.

Cumulative learning happens every time you read a business or technical document, when you learn how to use a new library, when you find the root cause of a bug or when you pair program with a teammate. This type of learning often occurs out of the need to solve a problem, you are not intentionally seeking to build a profound knowledge on the topic, you just need to know enough to get going with your work. Another aspect of cumulative learning is that it happens in a nonlinear fashion, you get pieces of information bit by bit from different experiences at different points in your career that aggregate into a bigger knowledge on a topic. The article you read, along with the discussion you had with a teammate and your practical experience compound to form knowledge. Another form of cumulative learning happens when you go to a conference. In this situation, the learning although more intentional is limited by how much can be taught in a 40-minute presentation. During conferences you are either deepening a little bit on a knowledge you already have or you are broadening your knowledge to areas you were not yet familiar with. In either situation, it's very likely that you'll need to get back into that topic later on in order to really consolidate it. Ideally you combine both passive and active types of cumulative learning on your routine. Besides going to conferences, another way to build that kind of knowledge is by following people on social media that are posting about your topics of interest and following newsletters. **Make it a goal to select one or two articles to read per week, use bookmarks or a tool that allows you to save content to read later and reserve some time in your week to go through the list.**

Conversely, specialization learning is a lot more intentional, focused, and deep. Specialization learning happens when you choose a topic to dedicate an extended amount of time, for example, when you read a book or when you sign into a course. In these situations, knowledge is built in a much more linear form, books and courses are planned to deliver the subject in an ordered way that is usually designed to optimize the learning. It's also expected that you are going to spend a considerable amount of time reflecting on the same topic before moving to a new one.

The challenge with specialization learning is that it's done with mid- and long-term goals in mind, there's normally no pressing issue to be solved by this new knowledge. Because of that, it requires a lot more discipline and active effort so people have an even harder time finding time in their agenda for it. It's possible to build an exceptional career based on cumulative learning but that usually depends a bit on being lucky, joining the right company at the right time, and meeting the right people. **By incorporating a routine of specialization learning, it's more likely that you will be able to control your next career steps and have more flexibility to pick what you want to do and where you want to work.** Knowing what your career goals are, make a prioritized list of topics you want to dig deeper into and include it in your routine of study. Although more tiring, specialization learning usually needs to be done outside of working hours, especially if you're investing in a topic that is not directly related to your job.

At the beginning of my career I decided to specialize in REST APIs and it was a decision that really paid off. It was a topic that was related to my day-to-day job and that I found interesting. I started by reading books on the subject and looking up blog posts. As I read stuff I also followed authors on social media and that helped me find other authors and more resources to deepen my knowledge. As I learned more I started sharing my knowledge first within my teammates, then writing blog posts and presenting in local conferences. I submitted talks and presented in bigger conferences and wrote a Python open source library that used RESTfull concepts to generate API clients. Even though the library was never hugely popular, it got some attention from the community and I got a talk approved to present it in Europe's largest Python conference. This whole process not only helped me grow as an engineer but it also served as a way to promote myself as a professional and to attract clients to Vinta.

As important as being strategic with your learning is not neglecting rest periods, as Will Larson, author of books on software engineering and management says, "pockets of rest enable careers." It's natural that sometimes your job is more demanding and that you have less energy for studying, sometimes it's a problem in your personal life that is making things harder and sometimes there's no clear motivation, you are just feeling tired. Taking a period of rest is good for your mind and for your body, don't stress out, consciously evaluate how you are feeling, let your body recover and plan your next steps. Constantly working at full capacity is not healthy and leads to burnout. **Plan your career for the long run, be intentional, build a sustainable flow and rest from time to time, ideally, way before you are close to your limit.**

Key takeaways:

- Leverage moments of high energy to grow faster, especially if you are starting in the career.

- Develop a routine of studying and self-development.

- Leverage cumulative learning to improve your current job performance.

- Leverage specialization learning to drive your long-term career growth.

- Don't forget to rest and respect your limitations, we are in this for the long run.

1.13 References and Further Reading

- "Using engineering principles to create autonomous teams at scale" by By Wayne Bell `https://leaddev.com/culture/using-engineering-principles-create-autonomous-teams-scale`

- "Know your "One Job" and do it first" by Charity Majors `https://charity.wtf/2021/03/07/know-your-one-job-and-do-it-first/`

- "Profit Centers vs Cost Centers at Tech Companies" by Gergely Orosz `https://newsletter.pragmaticengineer.com/p/profit-centers-cost-centers`

CHAPTER 2

Technical Discipline

© Filipe Ximenes 2024
F. Ximenes, *Strategic Software Engineering*, https://doi.org/10.1007/979-8-8688-0995-8_2

Every profession has a set of practices that, although not necessarily mandatory, are extremely important if professionals want to ensure exceptional results. Take, for example, the routine of a small independent restaurant chef, it might look something like this:

- Wake up early in the morning and go to the market to handpick the freshest available ingredients.

- Spend the afternoon washing vegetables, doing prep work, and making sure everything is ready for the day.

- In the evening, before customers arrive, she inspects the table setups to make sure everything looks beautiful and clean.

- As orders come in, she cooks the ingredients in a particular order and quantity, waiting the appropriate amount of time to extract the maximum flavor and producing the right texture.

- She carefully plates and examines each dish to ensure its presentation is visually appealing.

- At the end of the day, she ensures everything is cleaned up and ready for the next day.

Now, what happens if the chef wakes up late and all the fresh vegetables are already sold out? Would she still be able to cook? What if the table cloths are a bit dirty? Would customers notice? Would it hurt if she didn't invest as much in making glasses look shiny? In case any part of her routine goes bad, would she still be considered a chef? Yes, of course! Would customers have the same experience in her restaurant? I'm sure they wouldn't. The same applies to software, it's possible to develop bad software that works, just like a poorly prepared meal would still feed a person, but if you want to write great software there are some practices that will set you up for success. These practices are what we are going to be referring to as "discipline." They are often simple or easy to learn as concepts but are frequently not as easy to incorporate into a routine. Until you haven't got used to them and made them part of your day-to-day, they will feel burdensome. These practices normally require an active and intentional effort to change your mindset and you will often only perceive the benefits once they've become a natural part of your job. Examples of the software practices that fall under the umbrella of discipline are: writing automated tests and using Test Driven Development (TDD), writing documentation, refactoring, doing code reviews, and pair programming.

Something that is commonly misunderstood is *who* is accountable for discipline practices. Some engineers expect their companies to define what software development practices they expect from their employees, but that's not reasonable. The leadership of most companies are focused on business decisions, cash flow, sales, accounting, and human resources; they often don't understand the technicalities of building software, so we cannot expect them to know how to evaluate and decide what are the practices we should be following. It's our responsibility as qualified professionals to know the best practices and to apply them in our work. When software fails, engineers are the ones who are going to be blamed for it, so this is a responsibility that cannot be delegated to companies; engineers need to own it in order to build good software. By not adopting the right practices, engineers are risking the success of their work. This not only has consequences to the company they are working for but also to their own work life balance (such as pulling late nights fixing bugs or working on weekends) and to their long term career. Applying this logic to our previous example, you will notice that although it's up to the restaurant owner to provide the appropriate tooling and work environment, there are many parts of the job of a chef that the business either doesn't know about or cannot enforce. It's up to each individual to execute them.

Discipline is neither a technique nor a process. Technique describes how to execute an activity given a certain set of constraints (such as the available tools). For example, how to cut tomatoes using a chef's knife. Process defines a plan on how and when things are going to get executed, it might or might not give away the techniques that are expected to be employed. For example, a recipe on how to make pizza might tell you the ingredients and the order in which they should be mixed and cooked but it might not specify the technique on how to knead the dough. While process and technique can often be enforced, discipline needs to be nurtured from within us. It's possible to assess that a meal tastes delicious but it's [the cook's] discipline that ensures vegetables were properly cleaned before they were cooked.

One of the main impacts of discipline practices is related to the very nature of why we need software: its ability to change. Before software existed we already had machines [hardware] to automate things for us, but once they were built, it was not possible to change how they behaved. The revolution of the general purpose computer and software is the ability to change the machine behavior without the need to rebuild it. Change is what differentiates soft-ware from hard-ware. The very nature of software is to be changed and many of the discipline practices are there to help us build software that is easy to change. If we build software that is hard to change, we are defeating its purpose! We need to feel safe to change code without risking (or at least with the least possible risk of) breaking things. If this is not baked into how we perform our work, there's no way we can consistently deliver changeable software (good software!). Consistency is a keyword here. If we were writing software that was going to last for only a couple weeks and be thrown away or be replaced by a new one after that, there would be no reason to think about discipline. Discipline enables software that is more reliable, has fewer bugs, is easier to change, and that is more pleasant to work with. In the long run, this is what will allow us to deliver repeatedly and consistently. Lastly, discipline is about being reliable as engineers. If people know that you apply good practices and deliver consistently, they will trust you even when you eventually fail. They will know that it was probably a fluke or due to something that you could not control and are more likely to empathize with you. This has a direct impact on your customers, users, teammates, and also to your individual career.

The only way to really internalize discipline is by doing it. Practice it over and over until it's naturally part of your routine. If you are having trouble it's usually productive to bring these topics for discussion with fellow engineers and leaders. And remember there's no finish line, there's always something to learn or to improve, so find a pace that works for you, there's no need to rush.

2.1 Development Flow

One of the most basic applications of discipline is how we approach our day-to-day code assignments. This is not something we usually consciously think about but naturally everyone has their own sequence of steps they use in order to complete a programming task. The following items outline the main steps an experienced engineer will take while working on an assignment. Normally they won't be thinking about them as a sequence of steps nor will everyone agree on a correct order of execution, but most people will acknowledge that these steps reasonably match what they do. Here we are going to present them in an order that feels logical and that can be used as a practicing guideline. The idea is that you can repeat this process until it becomes ingrained in your mind and you don't have to think about it anymore. The goal of this exercise is to make you more conscious of your practices, thinking about each step as an isolated activity.

Understand the Business

First and foremost, make sure you understand what you are going to do. Carefully read the whole assignment, open and read any external documents referenced (docs, code snippets, ...), inspect diagrams, and study the design deliverables. If it's a change in an existing feature, play a bit with it, test different parameters and flows. Try to think from the perspective of the end user. How is it going to improve their life? Is there a better way of achieving the desired outcome? If necessary, ask questions and tag stakeholders. The main goal of this step is ensuring you are confident about what you have to do and that you have most of the information you need before starting. If you identify any gaps or missing information, consult with relevant stakeholders. If it's possible, do it asynchronously and move on to something else while you wait for what you need. If it's not possible to wait for answers, try other channels to reach out to people or schedule a quick meeting. Avoid context switching; if you start on something else, do not come back to the original task until you've finished the new one.

Understand the Code Context

Every feature exists in the context of a broader codebase and product. It's not possible to plan how you are going to write code if you don't understand the other parts of the software it will need to interact with. To do this, carefully read the whole flow where that code will be placed at and make sure you understand what is happening in each step. At this point there's no need to dig deeper into implementation details, just read the function/method/class names to get a broad understanding of the flow of the code. For example, if you are working on a web endpoint, start from the router, inspect the code that fetches data from the database, then the services being called, and finish with the content of the response. The solution to whatever you are trying to do needs to comply with how the system currently works so gathering this context is necessary in order to propose an adequate solution.

Plan a Solution

Now that you are confident about what you are going to do and the existing code linked to it, it's time to think about what your solution will look like. At this point you don't need to write any code. Just think it through, draw diagrams on paper, map relationships, sketch how things fit together, list all possible scenarios and states, and dig a little deeper into the existing code if you need more context. Once you have an initial idea, check if you are going to use any external libraries. If so, review the documentation to confirm it has the features you will need and that it behaves as you expect. Double-check if the library is well-maintained, and check open issues that might impact your work. Also check the library compatibility with your application (language version, framework version, licenses, etc.).

Now it's time to break down the solution in smaller blocks. As you do it, write these down as sub items. Think about edge cases, exceptions, integrations, and data validations. Also, check other functionalities that might be impacted or that will need more testing to confirm they weren't impacted. Also take note of these so you don't forget about them. Finally, consider all the non-functional aspects of the feature such as usability, performance, cost, data integrity, reliability, monitoring, and serviceability (we will talk more about non-functional requirements later in this chapter). If you are not sure about how these things can impact the production environment, ask someone with more context to help you with the analysis.

The last part of this planning is actually one of the most important: prioritizing the order activities will be tackled. To do this you need to evaluate the importance and risk of each activity and plan a "version zero." What is the minimum amount of work/activities you can do that delivers the most value? What is absolutely crucial to the final solution? What is less important and could be left for later? Here are some tips on how to evaluate risk:

- Is it time consuming? This can either indicate that it needs to move up or down in priority depending on how important it is. If it's time-consuming but critical, it's probably better to start from it.

- Can it become a blocker? Again it can either mean it needs to be moved up or down in priority depending on the importance. For example if it requires answers that are not yet at hand or if it depends on another piece of code before it can be done, perhaps you should leave it for latter. But if it can block other tasks from you or from your teammates, perhaps you should move it up on priority.

- If a task requires experience with a section of the code or a third party lib that you are not familiar with, it might be a good idea to give it a higher priority to avoid unforeseen blockers.

- Version zero can often be more forgiving with the UI, unless of course, it represents a risk for the feature value. For example, a complex animation that you don't have experience building.

While running this process you will often identify parts of the assignment that are too complex or time-consuming. When you notice this, try to imagine what other similar solutions would make things simpler or faster to build.

Validate Your Solution

For more complex features or if you are not confident about your solution, it's a good idea to validate it with someone else. In most cases a Tech Lead will be the best person to talk to because they have the technical context, but sometimes it can also be done with a manager, a designer, a peer, some other stakeholder. Write a paragraph or two explaining how you are planning to build the feature, including some but not all technical details, and send it for validation. If it's something that cannot be summarized in a couple paragraphs it might be a good idea to schedule a ten-minute desk-check to present and discuss your thoughts to streamline the process.

This is a good moment to report about risks, such as possible blockers or the complexity of the assignment. Confirm with stakeholders if a simpler solution you came up with works. Sometimes it will make sense to completely remove that complex part of the feature or delay it to another moment. Ensure any delayed features are registered in the issue tracker tool with proper context and information for it to be prioritized and addressed later.

Make It Work

Now it's time to start writing code. For now, focus only on the "version zero" you've defined. It's very important that you don't go beyond it. The goal is to have a working prototype that validates your assumptions. It's important to write the least code possible, you are still learning about how the new code fits in the existing one and validating the initial architecture we had in mind. Less code means it's easier to experiment with other approaches and to change the architecture in case you end up not liking the initial one. But don't go trying architectures until you have a working prototype. In fact, if it makes sense, consider writing this first version as a script completely detached from the application and then transplant it in.

Pace your work, don't get ahead of yourself. Because you've planned the execution you can, one by one, pick the topmost item in priority and work on them individually. Once you've picked an activity, focus on getting that single thing done and forget about any other tasks. Once you are done, commit the code and mark the item as completed, this is a small way to celebrate progress! Using Test Driven Development (TDD, more about it later in this chapter) will make this whole process much easier because it follows the same philosophy of gradual, paced work. It will also help you build a comprehensive test suite that will be essential in the next step, refactoring.

As you make progress you will identify unmapped edge cases and new requirements. It's important that you don't work on them immediately, simply add a new item to the list and prioritize it among the others; this will allow you to not deviate focus, reduce the cognitive load, and avoid getting anxious.

Refactor

With a working version zero it's time to invest on code quality and prepare the ground for a definitive solution. At this point you should not add any new features or fixes. Try architectures you think might better suit the problem, reorganize interfaces, rename variables, separate concerns, encapsulate implementation details, review if you are following the project code patterns, and make the code easy to read and clean. Because you've written tests you can be confident the work you've done so far works and that you are not breaking existing features as you refactor. Since you only have the bare bones of the feature, refactoring should require minimal effort. Once you are comfortable with the architecture and quality of the code, move on to the next step. (We will talk more about refactoring later on).

Fill in the Gaps

It's time to close up the solution. Work on the items you judged non-critical. Fill in the details, nice-to-haves', polish the interfaces, review how you are handling error and how you are managing edge cases. Keep the paced work, one task at a time, write automated tests, and celebrate progress by committing the new code and marking items as done. Review the code and check if you should add more log messages code comments.

Create and Update Docs

Finally, close the activity by checking if you need to create or update documentation. If applicable, consider how you are going to provide visibility to your team about the changes you've made. If it's a significant milestone, make sure to celebrate with your teammates by posting about it in a public channel or perhaps sharing a demo video of the new functionality.

2.2 Unblocking Flow

Getting blocked is a constant throughout the career of any software engineer, junior or senior, be it because of a hard-to-fix bug, or an integration that refuses to work. Blockers will always happen from time to time; what will change are your skills to get out of these situations. Just like in the "Development Flow," the unblocking flow is a suggested sequence of steps to practice being mindful, but this time to help you get unblocked. Most experienced engineers will not apply these techniques in a fixed predefined order but rather adapt to their context, parallelizing and adapting how much effort is spent depending on the situation. The steps are listed here in an order that balances the chances of success with the time and effort it takes. It should be used as a reference for practicing but it's encouraged that you experiment and find what works best for you in the context of your job. The general rule is to start from the less time-consuming and more effective approaches, and move on to more time-consuming methods.

Look for Similar Situations Within the Project

A common type of blocking situation is getting stuck with code that is not behaving as you expected. In this situation people often overlook the effectiveness of finding similar examples within the existing codebase.

Do some searching within the project and try to spot how tools are being used in other situations. Compare what you have with these other usage examples and try to compare them. You can also experiment tweaking both instances to become similar to each other and see if you can reproduce the issue. Use the debugger, set breakpoints, and inspect variables to gain more context.

Consult Your Preferred LLM

With AI tools getting ever more proficient on code, it makes sense to check early if they have an answer to your problem. When formulating your prompt, explain your problem providing some context such as the framework you are using, libraries and APIs, describe the problem to the best of your knowledge, include snippets of code and stack traces if available. Try a few prompts exploring different aspects of the issue or reformulating how you frame the problem. Prompting a LLM is often productive and can provide great insights, but be careful with just copy pasting code. Although just trying out whatever these tools spit is a good way to find a solution to your problem, your work shouldn't end there. Don't waste this opportunity to really understand what fixed the problem and why your initial attempts didn't work. Once you have working code, make tweaks to see how changing it affects the software, inspect variables and test different parameters. That kind of exploration is a great way to deepen your understanding and it pays off in the long term. Another way to leverage these situations is to read the documentation for the tools the LLM used to solve the problem. This is important as a way to double-check the information you were given (LLMs are prone to hallucinating) and to learn more about the tools you are using. Even when AI gives the wrong answers they can still be useful because they can expand your vocabulary which you can use to improve your prompts and search queries. After a few tries if the suggestions are not effective, move on to the old-school alternatives.

Quick Search on the Internet

If the LLMs don't work, then try doing a quick search on the Internet. At this point, you should only be trying to rule out if the problem is trivial and if it has already been solved. Try multiple search queries and scan through the first couple pages of results, don't go further. When you click on an article, first scan through it to confirm it has potential. If it does, do read the whole thing, try not to just skim over the information; you might not find the solution there but you will probably gain context about things related to your problem. Consider checking the project issue tracker if it's related to an open source library. Here are some tips on how to write search terms on Google:

- Use the terms you see in the console such as exceptions and log messages.

- Don't use (or remove from logs) project-specific terms, like file paths, class/method/function/ names.

- Experiment with broader and more specific terms.

- Restrict search to a domain; for example, "site:stackoverflow.com," "site:github.com".

As a reference, don't spend more than 20 minutes in this phase.

Double-Check Your Mental Models

Mental models are how you organize your existing knowledge to form an expectation about how things work. For example, most people don't know the details about how a hydroelectric power plant works, but if you were asked about it you could probably make some guesses that will seem coherent to you. **When we are programming we are constantly using mental models to make projections about how we expect the code we write to behave. It's impossible to know all the details of what is going**

on under the hood of all the software tools we use, so mental models allow us to fill in the gaps without the need to actually know everything. The problem is that our assumptions don't always match reality leading to false expectations and a seemingly coherent but incorrect understanding about what is going on. To prevent getting stuck in this situation, you need to let go of some of these assumptions, double-check your knowledge, and rebuild your mental models.

Reach Out to the Team

Write a paragraph explaining what you are doing, the issues you are facing, and share in the internal company channels. Explain what approaches you have tried so far, provide code samples and link to parts of the codebase that would help people understand what you are talking about. You can use the team channels or the company-wide channels if there's one that can be used for this purpose. While you wait for an answer move on to other approaches.

Read the Docs

At this point, it's reasonable to assume you might be dealing with a non-trivial issue. Since it looks like not many other people have gone through the issue, you'll need to deepen your knowledge on the subject in order to develop the skills to solve it. Look for available documentation on the tools you are using, find the section that covers what you are trying to do, and read it from top to bottom. You will be amazed how much you will learn by doing this; not only will it help you fix the current issue but it will also give you useful insights for your future self. Docs are mostly used for one-of consultation but there's so much they can provide if you dedicate a bit more to them.

Go Deeper Into the Code

If docs don't help, it's probably worth investing some time reading the code of the tool you are using. Start from higher levels of abstraction and inspect the inner workings of it going deeper as you see fit. Review what parameters are available and how data flows through methods. This is yet another opportunity to learn as you will be able to see the architecture and patterns other developers used to build that tool.

Seek External Help

If the previous approaches didn't work, you might need external help. For commercial tools open a ticket in their support channel, for open source check if there's an issue tracker in the repository or if there's a forum, email list, or chat channel you can talk to other users and maintainers of the library. Consider asking a question on a public technology forum. In all cases, do provide as much context as possible, but try to abstract business details that are not relevant for the situation. Make your text short and easy to understand in order to increase the chances of getting an answer. For the common scenario this step is left as one of the last resources as it's not always available and it usually takes a considerable amount of time to receive answers (if they ever do). For that same reason, this is one of the things you should do in an urgent or critical situation, post your message and move on to other things as you wait for an answer.

Debug the Source Code [If It's Available]

If nothing works, it's time to bring up the big guns. Dig into the source code of the tool you are trying to use but this time trying to debug it. Set up breakpoints and make changes to the code to better understand the inner workings of it and test what would need to change in order for you accomplish what you want. Copy and paste code blocks related to what you are doing into your own code so you can more easily test changes.

2.3 Bug-Fixing Flow

Fixing bugs is an integral part of every engineer's life to the point that often we don't think much about the process of doing it. Indeed it's possible to jump into the code, change a few lines and get the problem fixed, but by being systematic we can make our solutions more consistent and reliable. The goal of this flow is to propose a sequence of steps that will lead you to not only fixing bugs but also doing it in a safe, well planned way and with minimal risks.

1. Understand the Problem and the Context

First and foremost, make sure you understand the problem. Carefully read the bug report, related assets, the context, and the parameters that caused it. If necessary, ask questions to help getting a clear understanding about the issue. You should have clear answers to both these questions:

- How is the system supposed to work?

- How is the system currently behaving?

2. Reproduce

Now that you understand the problem it's time to reproduce the bug. This seems obvious but sometimes we receive a bug report and get straight into fixing it even before seeing it happens for ourselves. This is dangerous behavior because it can lead to misunderstandings of the problem and even situations where we fix (or break) other parts of the system that are not what was initially reported. Once you reproduce it, the next step is to identify what is causing it. Although this step can sometimes be done by using the system, the best way to reproduce a bug in a consistent way is to write a regression test.

3. Write a Regression Test

A regression test is an automated unit or integration test that captures a bug. It must be written before any alteration in the application code is made. The goal is to have a test that breaks precisely due to the bug you are investigating. Once you have a failing test you can then write the code that fixes the bug and run the test again to confirm it passes. The rationale is that by isolating the bug in a test and only changing the minimum amount of code required to make it pass you can confidently ensure your solution is what is fixing the issue. The advantages of this process include confirming you've correctly found the root cause, isolating the issue in a controlled environment, being able to quickly and automatically assess your solution works (the test is passing), and adding a permanent automated test in your test suite that asserts this particular bug won't be introduced again later on.

4. Find the Root Cause

Debugging is the practice of tracing what is causing a bug; just because you know which parameters make the system break it does not mean that you know what in the code is causing it to break. A key factor in debugging is ensuring that you fully understand what the problem is before you start trying to fix it. You should never start working on a complex solution unless you are confident that you've found what is the root cause of the problem. In the next section, we will cover some techniques that can help with this process of debugging.

5. Fix the Bug

Now that you know what is the cause of the problem and that it's "captured" in a test you can work on the final solution to fix it. While working on a bug it's common to find other problems in the code you would like to fix or change, avoid this temptation. In software development, change always means risk, and we don't want to risk introducing other bugs as we try to fix the initial one. Make sure you write the least amount of code and that this code only affects the part of the system that you are fixing. Other changes that aren't directly related to the bug should be delivered separately, with dedicated attention, planning, and testing.

2.4 Debugging Techniques

In the previous section, we discussed a basic flow that leads to effectively fixing bugs, but we haven't actually presented how to actually debug. While there's no silver bullet and each engineer develops their own methods and preferences as they practice and gain experience, there are certainly a few common ground techniques that usually lead to good results. In this section, we are going to explore some of these techniques and how they can be employed to make your debugging more strategic. As usual, experiment and practice with these to build your own toolbox that you can pick and choose depending on the situation.

Add Breakpoints [or Print Statements]

Most programming languages are fitted with debuggers, tools that allow you to set up breakpoints to intercept the execution of a code and inspect the state of variables. Similar results can also be achieved (with a little more work) by adding print statements. While both approaches are fine and you should use whatever you feel more comfortable with, debuggers usually offer a set of features like "stepped execution" that are very handy. The usual approach is to set up the breakpoints and run the software to trigger them, but it's sometimes more effective to set up an automated test or to write a script that reproduces the issue you are investigating. That way it's easier to change parameters, making it a lot more effective to run it multiple times until you find the issue.

Debuggers are a dividing topic among engineers, some are very fond of them and acknowledge them as powerful tools for tracing problems but many do just fine using print statements. Even if you prefer to use print statements, it's worth the investment to get acquainted with debuggers and have this skill in your toolbox. It's certain that from time to time you will stumble upon situations where they are a lot more effective.

Read the Stack Trace

Most programming languages will print some form of stack traces when they encounter an execution problem. These are usually the first place you should look at when trying to understand what went wrong. Stack traces may seem a bit messy at first glance, but with practice, you will get used and your eyes will quickly be drawn to the important bits. The first thing you should do when you see a stack trace is to confirm it matches your expectations. Confirm the execution went through the methods you expected it to. If you are working with a language that has support for exceptions they will be shown in the trace and that's often the best place for you to start your investigation. Frequently a quick search on the web or prompting a LLM about these will give you a few good pointers to what is the problem or at least what should be the next steps in your investigation.

When reading stack traces pay especial attention to the points where it transitions between layers such as internal language methods, framework code, third party libraries, and your application. Start focusing on the things that are closer to the application code and dig your way to lower level layers as you see necessity.

Change One Thing at a Time

When debugging, you are trying to find the root cause of a bug so it's important that you keep track of what you are doing or it will not be possible to determine how or which changes to the code impact the results. By being incremental you can gradually work your way toward the root cause without opening too many simultaneous branches of exploration. The general rule is: if it helps getting you closer to reproducing or fixing the bug, keep it; otherwise, undo the change so it won't affect your next experiments. Notice that for this to work effectively, it should be supported by an automated regression test so you can quickly run the code multiple times.

Comment Things Out

A good way to track down what is causing a problem is to "reduce the scope." The idea is to comment parts of the code until the error stops showing up. At this point you start uncommenting line-by-line until the error shows up again. Start from high level code, once you've pinpointed what line causes the problem to change or to go away you can uncomment it and repeat the process in level down (inside that method). Keep repeating that process and it's likely that you will end up finding the exact line that is causing the problem.

Compare Similar Parts of the Code

As mentioned before, comparing the broken code with other similar parts of the project can be very insightful. Look for the differences between the two blocks of code and try to reproduce the issue in the one that is supposedly working as expected. It's likely that you will either find out that both flows are suffering from the same issue or identify what difference is causing one to work but not the other.

Write a Simplified Version of the Feature

Sometimes it is just better to throw everything out and start over. Instead of deleting your application code you can simulate that by writing a separate, simplified script with the minimum amount of code to reproduce what you are trying to achieve. Make it in a way that is easy to tweak parameters and run it again so you can iterate faster. This method is a great way to isolate the problem and confirm your mental model matches reality. Once you get your "toy" version running as expected you can then transplant it back to the application code making the necessary adaptations. Don't forget to write a regression test before you start changing your application code, all its benefits are still valid and worthwhile in this context.

Rubber Duck Debugging

You'd be surprised by how effective it is to just explain your problem to someone else as a way to find what is causing it. The process of formulating the issue in a way another person will understand it and have enough context to help you out forces your brain to organize the information and review your knowledge base often leading to insightful conclusions. The rubber duck debugging method consists of using a rubber duck (or any plastic figure of your preference) and explaining the problem to it, sometimes all you need is someone to talk to. In case you don't have a rubber duck at your disposal, a teammate should work just fine as a replacement.

Pair Programming

If you explain the issue to an inanimate object and it refrains from helping you, it might be a good idea to invite a human being for a pair programming session. Make sure you give as much context as possible and list the things you've tried so far (we will talk more about pair programming later on).

Record Your Findings

As your debugging progresses, write down the things you've experimented with so far as a way to track what you already tried. Include information about the experiments you've tested, which tools and commands you've used, what produced insightful results, and what were the dead-ends. You can use these notes for your own tracking but they are also useful for giving context for teammates in case you need their help later on. These notes can be later posted in a team wiki or in the issue tracker for further reference in case a similar problem shows up in the future.

2.5 Refactoring

In simple terms, refactoring is the act of restructuring code while not adding or changing functionality. **Code design has a natural tendency to gradually fall apart over time which, compounded by pressure to deliver fast, results in what is often referred to as technical debt. The main goal of refactoring is paying back technical debt and with that, keep the codebase easy and safe to be changed.** That all translates into value added to the business through faster feature delivery, less overall bugs, code that is easier to maintain (and bugs that are easier to fix), a product that is more reliable and stable, engineers that are more productive and happier with their work, and ultimately, happier customers.

The biggest blocker engineers have when it comes to refactoring is thinking that it requires big architectural changes. This is actually far from reality as refactoring can be as simple as renaming a variable to a more comprehensive term. All engineers, even the most novice ones, should feel empowered to make improvements to the codebase as they identify opportunities. Don't make a big deal of it, keep in mind that your leaders only expected you to refactor up to your level of experience using the toolset you are already comfortable with. As small as they might seem, any improvements to the codebase should be celebrated and acknowledged as a step toward a better codebase.

Once you break that initial barrier and start doing more refactorings you might notice that there are some pitfalls that you should avoid. One of the main risks for inexperienced engineers when refactoring is to lose track of what their goals are and the amount of time they use. When you start changing too many things at once, it's quite easy to mess it up to an irreparable point where it's hard to even get things back to the original state. It's also not uncommon to accidentally invest too much time on a refactoring that turns out to be a dead-end or on a low priority issue that ends up delaying your main assignments. It's important that you learn to identify these traps in order to avoid accidentally falling into them and setting some guardrail rules. What will make you comfortable and effective with refactoring is practice and experimentation, so here are some guidelines that you can use to develop this skill:

1. First identify the part of the application where you believe code can be improved.

2. Make a checkpoint commit in your version control system that you can revert back to in case things don't go according to the plan.

3. Set a 20-minute timer.

4. Start refactoring and remember that you should not add or modify existing feature behavior; your only goal should be to improve the code without affecting how it behaves.

   a. Read the code and as you understand what it's doing add comments; these can be temporary just to help you through the process, but later on you might decide to keep them if you think they are useful to other engineers.

   b. Start with small and easy things such as renaming
      variables, functions and classes.

   c. Try moving related code close to each other.

   d. Try extracting blocks of code into self-contained
      functions or classes.

   e. Experiment with alternative architectures.

5. When the timer ends, you will then decide how to
   proceed:

   a. If you like how things are going, estimate how long
      it will take to finish the refactoring and if it fits your
      schedule keep going. Set another timer to your new
      estimation so you don't lose track of time and risk
      your other deliveries.

   b. If you think you are not making good progress or
      that you are heading toward a dead-end, revert
      the changes and move back to your assignments.
      Perhaps you can think more about the issue and try
      again in another moment.

When using these guidelines it doesn't matter if you will complete the
refactoring or not, the main goal of this exercise is to practice, lose the fear
of changing code, and experimenting with your ideas. Force yourself to
think about ways to improve the code for the entire 20 minutes, even if you
feel stuck do not give up. Keep in mind that even if you make no progress
you are only "wasting" 20 minutes, it's not a big deal. Try to do this one or
two times per week until you get used to the process, soon enough your
brain will start to automatically spot refactoring opportunities and it will
be a natural part of your workflow.

Refactoring is a concept that is easy to explain to non-technical business people as it makes logical sense, but, at the same time, it's frequently hard to get the buy-in from higher-ups because they will often perceive it as trading new features for a hard-to-estimate and distant benefit. The contradiction is that, later on, when the cost of shipping features rises and things start to break, engineers will be the ones to blame for letting that happen. The best way to avoid this situation is to treat refactoring for what it is, a discipline that is part of the ongoing operation of writing software and like so there's no need to bargain time for refactoring, you just do it as an integral part of your job writing software. There's no need to distinguish what is feature development and what is refactoring, instead you should be continuously doing small improvements to the code around the features you are working on.

Although the main goal is always to improve existing code, there are a few different contexts where refactoring can be applied. Martin Fowler, writer o many books about software development, divides them into six categories; knowing their differences is useful in order to strategically plan how you are going to act:

- Test Driven Development (TDD): This is the conventional TDD flow, Red ➤ Green ➤ Refactor (we will talk more about TDD later on).

- Litter Pickup: While on TDD, you are refactoring something that you just wrote; on litter pickup, you are refactoring something that you stumbled upon while browsing the code or working on a task. It's the girl/boy scouts rule: always leave it cleaner than you found it.

- Comprehension: Sometimes we will stumble upon a piece of code that requires a more careful reading before we fully understand what it's doing. While this is a good sign that this code would benefit

from a refactoring, if you don't have the time to
do it immediately, you can at least write a few
code comments or improve the naming of variables
and methods. The goal of this type of refactoring is to
help the next person understand the code quicker than
you have.

- Preparatory: Some code might seem fine, until you
  need to add or change something in it. In this situation,
  it's often a good idea to first refactor it, preparing it for
  the change before you actually work on the new feature.
  This is one of the few situations where refactoring pays
  off immediately.

- Planned: This is when blocks of refactoring are added
  to a backlog and prioritized along with all the features.
  The danger of it is that it's hard to measure the value
  of a refactoring especially when comparing it to a
  feature so it's easy for it to keep getting postponed. If
  this kind of refactoring is happening often, it might
  mean the team is not doing enough of the other types
  of refactoring.

- Long Term: As the codebase gets older, some parts will
  build cruft that cannot be fixed in a single sit-down
  session. When this happens, the best idea is to break
  down the task into small steps that lead to the final goal
  but that do not need to be tackled all at once.

In the end, the ideal way to think about refactoring is doing small
changes that over time compound to big improvements. It's inevitable
that from time to time your team will need to plan dedicated time in the
backlog to work on larger issues but that should not be the norm.

Key takeaways:

- Refactoring is about improving the codebase to enable better-performing teams and products.

- All improvements to the code are worthy and welcome no matter how small they seem.

- Make refactoring a part of your day-to-day job as an engineer, long-term gains usually come from continuous small improvements.

- Be mindful about the time investment so refactoring doesn't impact roadmap activities.

2.6 Refactoring Patterns

Some patterns are clear indicators of refactoring opportunities; knowing about them will allow you to address problems early on, improving the quality of the code before cruft grows. There are many such patterns, here we are going to list some that are easy to identify and that can help you start practicing your refactoring skills.

Improve Naming

This is one of the simplest forms of refactoring as it simply consists of changing the name of variables, functions, methods, classes, and modules. Remember that the goal of writing clean code is to improve the work of our fellow engineers; computers just follow instructions, they don't care about architecture or good practices. The nature of code is that it's written once and read many times so every opportunity we have to make the codebase easier to understand is time well invested and it pays off in the long term. J.B. Rainsberger describes four stages of naming as

1. Nonsense

2. Accurate-but-vague

3. Precise

4. Meaningful or intention-revealing

Every time you promote names between stages, you are significantly improving the code.

Rule of Three

The rule of three, as describe by Martin Fowler in the book Refactoring, states that you should wait until you repeat something for the third time before you create an abstraction (and refactor everything to use the new abstraction). The rationale behind this is that the first time you write a piece of code is the moment you have the least context about the problem you are working on. Therefore, even if you expect that it should be designed as a generic abstraction that can be reused multiple times, it's premature to do so. You shouldn't try to predict the future, instead wait until you have actually written similar code a few times, gathering more information and context about the problem before you can better design a generic solution that fits all cases.

Principle of Proximity

The Principle of Proximity, popularized by Adam Tornhill, states that "code that changes together should be moved closer." It's only natural that as software grows code will end up misplaced; this usually happens as people gradually add new code focusing on completing their own task without giving proper attention to the bigger context and architecture. It's easy to notice when this kind of pattern emerges: when working on a feature, you will either notice that you are constantly jumping between files that are positioned too far apart or that you have to scroll up and down too much on a large file. If either of these are happening, it's a sign that you might benefit from moving code closer together. This can be done in multiple ways such as reorganizing file structure, moving code from one file to another, and grouping together classes and methods that interact with each other in the same file.

Leveling Abstraction

Sometimes it's possible to make code easier to read by grouping (chunking) blocks and moving them up a level of abstraction, placing it in a self-contained method, for example. When programming, we aim to create layers of abstraction that allows other engineers reading the code to quickly have an overall understanding from looking at higher level abstractions but still allowing them to easily delve into the details for more context. Large blocks of uninterrupted code, such as a method with more than 50 lines for a reference, are likely mixing code that should be in different levels of abstraction. To fix this you can move the code inside the method into multiple self-contained methods that will be called from the original one. The originally large method will end up with just a few lines of code that simply call other [well named] methods. Now when someone needs to read this method, it will be much faster and easier to get an overall understanding of what it's doing. With a quick glance engineers can now grasp an initial understanding of what the code does, which will be enough for most of the time and only if they really need more detailed information about how it works they will dig down into the lower level abstractions.

Highlight the Success Path

Clear software has a single success path, this means a couple things. First, it means that any given method should have a single and clear purpose. One of the ways to identify if you are doing this correctly is when naming that block of code; if it's hard to give it a simple name that conveys what it's doing, you've got a sign something might be wrong. Second, it means that the method's success path (or happy path) is not nested. Methods usually include code for data validation, error handling, and side effects, although these are all very important, they are not the main reason the method exists. The success path is the sequence of steps for when everything happens according to the plan and the main goal of that code is successfully executed. Code that is deep down into control statements, such as if/else and try/catch clauses or for loops, is considered "nested" and is usually harder to read. Ideally the success path of our methods should be placed with as little nesting as possible. One of the main techniques to achieve this are guard clauses; if you are not familiar with this concept, it's well worth looking it up. In summary, to highlight the success path you should have methods with a single purpose and with a flat (or unnested) success path.

2.7 Automated Tests

One of the first things all engineers will learn early on in their careers is the direct correlation between changing code and it breaking. Computers are built to precisely reproduce the instructions they are given so, unless the parameters change, they should return the exact same result no matter how many times you run a program. We know that this statement is not always true as in practice hardware can fail and having software that always runs with the same exact parameters is not very useful. But this statement is insightful because we can derive from it that the riskiest moment in the software development process is when we change code. And I'm sad to give you the bad news: your job is to keep changing code, and I guarantee that you will break things from time to time. If changing code is an inherent risk to our profession, testing is our main weapon to fight against it.

Testing is inevitable because either you do it or your users will do it for you. The most basic form of testing a feature is just using it in the same way you expect your users to. Suppose that to prevent bugs you decide to test all the features of your system before deploying any new changes to your users. The problem with this idea is that features don't exist in a vacuum, they are built to interact with each other. In the moment you connect two separate pieces of code, you are creating dependency, meaning that they can now interfere with each other. Now your changes in one part of the system can potentially generate bugs in the other part that was previously isolated. Keep adding new features and shortly the amount of interconnections become exponentially bigger and adding a single line of code requires weeks of testing before it can be deployed. The good news is that as software engineers we are specialists in automating repetitive tasks, we can fight software with software! Notice that's not to say that manual testing doesn't have its place, on the contrary, it's very useful in some contexts and even essential for many industries, but even in these situations, they are more effective when done in combination with automated tests.

Automated tests can be categorized in a spectrum that goes from testing a small isolated function to simulating a human clicking through an interface. Although there are many subdivisions, the three main categories are unit, integration, and end-to-end tests. Unit tests are focused on testing small blocks of code in an isolated manner, meaning it should not depend on any shared resource or interact with anything external to the program itself, such as a database or even the file system. Everything is done "in memory" and because of that these tests are expected to run very fast. To write pure unit tests for code that makes database queries or web API calls, you need to replace these by "test doubles" that simulate the behavior of these services without actually calling them.

The next category in the spectrum are the integration tests; its purpose is to ensure that interconnected blocks of code or systems touching each other are behaving correctly. While unit tests run in an isolated environment where state is never persisted, integration tests are expected to have actual interactions with external systems. For example, if a method saves data in the database, the test should be able to query the database and assert the date actually there. Because of that nature it's not wise to use the same environment of your production application to run these tests as it could easily generate inconsistent data or risk corrupting data from users. The solution is to set up a separate test environment with a configuration that matches your production environment as closely as possible. One downside for this, is that, although your test environment uses the same or similar technologies as your production environment, it's not populated with real user data which is not always easy to reproduce. If your test data is too simplified, there's a good chance that your tests will not pick up on problems that require more complex scenarios to show up. The data used to pre-populate a test environment is commonly referred to as "fixtures." There are techniques that can help with the setup of text fixtures. For instance, there are tools that can help you to automatically generate random data. It's also possible to use a copy of the production data as fixtures (as long as user data is anonymized to prevent security issues). There are pros and cons to each approach but most programming languages have tools to assist with this task, it pays off to do some research and get familiarized with the ones available in your stack. Keep in mind that integration tests are noticeably slower than unit tests, as accessing data through the network or from a file storage is naturally orders of magnitude slower than accessing memory.

In the last category are the end-to-end (E2E) tests and these are by far the slowest and more expensive to write and maintain. The goal of end-to-end testing is to write software that uses the system just like an end user would. Objectively, end-to-end testing is the best kind of automated testing as it truly verifies how the system behaves from the most important perspective, the user's. It does not care about what language the software was written on, or what algorithms are under the hood, it only matters what the interface shows, that's why it's considered a *black box* test just like a manual test performed by a human being. Unit and integration tests break through the user interface abstraction and have access to things that the user is not directly exposed to. Being able to use the system just like end users comes with a high cost. Automated end-to-end tests are much harder to set up, to write, and to maintain. They are also a lot slower and often considered too brittle as they can fail due to small changes in the user interface that do not necessarily indicate a problem. But, for that same reason they have the advantage of being very effective at capturing subtle bugs that otherwise could pass unnoticed and they are resilient to big code architecture changes as they don't care about the inner workings of the software.

Notice that accessing resources outside of your local network is usually, and preferably, out of the scope for unit and integration tests. External API calls, for instance, are yet a few orders of magnitude slower than querying a database located in the same machine as the test runner. There's the issue of consistency and reliability as automated tests should not be subjected to downtime and instability from an external service provider. And there's also the complexities of setting up test data in an environment that is not in your full control. In these situations automated tests are better used just as validators of the contracts between systems. In most situations there's no need to make external calls in your automated tests, focus on verifying that you are calling the right URL and passing the parameters correctly.

After learning about these three categories and their pros and cons, the next step is practicing when to employ each type of test. As always the answer will greatly vary depending on factors such as the type of system you are working on, its criticality, scale, maturity, number of engineers working on it, size, and even the tech stack you are using. That said, there's a framework called *the test pyramid* that it's widely accepted as a good reference to guide automated tests. At the bottom of the pyramid are the unit tests; these are the cheapest type of tests to write and the fastest to run so you can have a lot of them. On top of it, a bit more complex to setup and slower to run are the integration tests, so you are a bit more cautious with it. Try to cover most of the business logic with unit tests and only use integration tests to check the interaction between components. Some business logic requires integration tests, such as in situations where there are side effects like sending emails or sending data to an external API. Whenever possible, use abstractions that allow testing these integrations within your local machine, for example, you can set up a fake email server that receives the connection and confirms the integration is working but that does not actually send an email. End-to-end tests are on the top of the test pyramid, as the slowest and most expensive of all three, they should be used cautiously. It's often wise to only cover the most critical application flows with end-to-end tests instead of trying to catch everything there. Also because they are so slow it's usually a good idea to run them separately from the other types of tests and perhaps leave them to the end of the pipeline so they only run after all the others are successful.

Besides confirming that new code does what it's expected to do and developing a solid foundation that ensures old features don't break as you add new ones, tests can also be used as documentation. They describe what each feature is supposed to do and, in a way, they are better than text documentation as they are self-correcting, letting you know when something gets outdated, which is a thing normal docs are known to perform poorly. When you start working on a part of the codebase you are not familiar with, try first reading its tests to acquire context about how it works and what are the available features and parameters. If the tests are well written, they will give you a lot of context not only on the goals of that feature but also on side effects and edge cases that would be hard to learn from just reading the code. Treating tests as docs will also help you write better tests. Just like any other code, tests should be written for a computer to execute but also for our fellow engineers to learn and keep them updated as the system evolves. Keep them organized, easy to find, and grouped by feature, use comprehensive and self-explanatory names and descriptions. Just like in any other code, small blocks are much easier to understand. At the same time don't be afraid of being descriptive or verbose, we want tests to be as simple and as easy as possible to read and understand. Add code comments to your tests whenever you feel they are going to help other team members.

Another benefit of automated tests is to reduce anxiety and cognitive load for the team. **Software should be easy and safe to change, by keeping an extensive suite of tests you are making your job a lot less stressful.** One key benefit is that they allow you to safely work on parts of the code that you are not familiar with, knowing that there will be a safety net that prevents you from making a catastrophic mistake. This enables you to work focused on the task at hand because you can passively wait for the test suite to inform you that something is wrong rather than actively trying to think about all possible ways your changes can break existing features. Of course no amount of tests will ever guarantee that software won't break, but with less context to account for you can keep a paced work thinking about one thing at a time. By reducing the anxiety of changing code, automated tests enable a team that is not afraid of refactoring and that can fix bugs and add new features safely and considerably faster.

It's important to think about the developer experience of the test suite if we want to keep it relevant in the long term. If it's not enjoyable, people will gradually stop caring about it, causing a snowball effect that can quickly escalate and lead to abandonment. The number one factor of discontentment with tests in a team is speed, so whenever you feel tests are taking too long to run, invest some time on improving the speed of your test suite. There are various techniques available to address this, so do some research on what is available within your tech stack. Make sure it's easy to run a single test or a section of the test suite, it's very frustrating and unproductive if one needs to frequently run the full test suite while working on a specific feature. In fact, engineers should rarely need to run the full test suite themselves, that job should be delegated to a Continuous

Integration (CI) tool that automatically verifies everything before new code is allowed to be merged into the main codebase. Test coverage tracking tools are good allies helping teams to develop a culture of writing tests and ensuring they don't let the ball drop. These tools measure what's the percentage of the codebase that is currently covered by at least one test so you can track progress and set a bar that the team needs to keep up with. Although these tools provide a good reference metric, they should be used carefully as they tell nothing about the quality of tests; just because the test suite touches some part of the code does not mean the tests are actually ensuring it is behaving well. For that same reason it's usually not productive to set the bar too high; 100% test coverage does not guarantee anything and it's often an unreasonable goal. For most projects, somewhere between 75% to 90% coverage is good enough. But don't forget, the quality of your test suit is much more important than any coverage metric or even the total number of tests you have.

Despite still not being the norm for every engineer, from small startups to big corporations (with very few exceptions due to scale contexts), automated tests are an industry standard for every mature development team. These teams don't write automated tests because they think it's cool, they do it because it's cheaper, faster, and more effective than not writing them. **Strategic engineers make automated tests an integral part of their job and deeply care about the amount and the quality of the tests they write as well as invest into making test suite's execution easy and enjoyable for everyone.** In order to be effective, tests need to be a collective endeavor for the whole engineering team.

Key takeaways:

- Be mindful about the test pyramid and the architecture of your test suite in order to optimize coverage, maintainability, and speed.

- Beyond validating the correctness of code, tests can also be used as live documentation.

- Leverage automated tests to reduce the cognitive load and the anxiety of changing code, allowing teams to move faster.

- To increase adhesion and promote usage, ensure that tests are easy and fast to run.

2.8 Test-Driven Development (TDD)

Test-Driven Development, or TDD as it's popularly known, is a methodology that uses tests for guiding software development. Contrary to the common misconception, it's not a methodology to write tests, **the goal is to improve the quality of the code you write with a side effect of producing a robust test suite in the process.** The TDD methodology defines a cycle with three steps RED → GREEN → REFACTOR:

- Red: Start by writing one (and only one) test that asserts a small piece of the functionality you are developing. Since the functionality does not exist the test will obviously fail. This first step must end when you run the test and confirm it fails.

- Green: Write the smallest possible code that will make the test you just wrote to pass. At this point do not worry about making the code look good or performant, just focus on making the test pass.

- Refactor: Now that you have working software and a test that confirms it, refactor it to a cleaner or more performant form. Remember that *refactoring* implies no functionality is added or removed.

- Repeat: Pick another part of the functionality and start over the cycle.

This process is simple enough and easy to remember but it carries a bunch of insights and benefits to the software development process. For starters, TDD reduces the anxiety of working with big features. Instead of trying to write a full solution to the problem, you can calm down and focus on smaller parts of it. You just need to write enough code to make the test pass, focus on that single thing, then move on to another small thing and before you notice it you will have a complete solution. As you repeat the cycle you will gradually build a robust test suite that backs up all the work you've done and therefore there's far less risk of accidentally breaking things as you move. Another key factor is that by ensuring the test first fails and only writing enough code to make it pass, you are ensuring that the code you wrote does exactly what it was intended for and it's what is making the test pass. Knowing that you already have a working solution, you take away a significant portion of the pressure and can progressively refactor up to the point where you are satisfied with. Also, because you end up with many tests, each focused on a small section of your code, when something breaks your test suite will point right away where the problem is.

You're likely to find the first few attempts at TDD challenging. It will possibly seem unnatural or boring. Until you get used to it you will need a bit of faith, your mind will eventually adapt to it and you will start noticing the benefits. Do not give up, keep forcing yourself, it should pay off eventually. One of the things that will help in this process is the feedback loop, the sense of continuously making progress. Nevertheless, one caveat of this process is that it will only work if you keep these cycles short. If the test suite takes too long to run or if you write tests that require too much code to pass, the magic won't work. It's rewarding to strike through a bunch of quick wins, you will feel happy and productive with your work, and that's what's going to make you fall in love with TDD. Remember, TDD is a tool like any other, learn how to use it so it's available to be employed when you see fit.

Key takeaways:

- Respect the TDD cycle: RED ➤ GREEN ➤ REFACTOR.

- Make cycles short, write a test that asserts a small
  progress and write the least amount of code to make
  it pass.

- Focus first on making it work, and later, in the refactor
  phase, make it better.

- Give TDD some time to settle before you understand
  the flow and it starts making sense.

2.9 Reviewing Teammates' Code

In most mature teams, it's standard practice to have a rule that no code
goes to production without being reviewed by at least one engineer other
than the author or the code. There are some methodologies that are based
on this rule with slightly different ways of achieving it and each company
will have their own set of policies. The most popular way of implementing
it is through "pull requests," which is how Github calls their code review
tool, but there are other approaches. For instance, one interesting way
(but much less popular) is requiring engineers to always be working in
pairs. In this and in the next sections we will be talking about the process
of peer reviewing code, first by addressing how you can be strategic
when looking at someone else's code and then how you can improve
the way you submit your own code for others to review. As it's not fully
standardized across companies, notice that in this book we will use the
word "merge" to describe the process of integrating new code (or any
kind of changes) to a codebase. "Merge request" will be used to describe
the process of submitting code for peer review. And we will use the word

"push" to describe the process of sending the code changes you made in your machine to a common repository where it will be available to other engineers.

The first thing to keep in mind is that a **reviewer owns the code they are reviewing as much as the person who wrote it.** In fact that should be your attitude toward everything in the product (we will discuss more about this later in the *Strategic Teamwork* chapter). One of the goals of the code review process is to share risks. As a reviewer you are as accountable for a bug that goes to production as the engineer who originally wrote the code. Don't think of code review as a secondary chore; really get involved as if it was your own code because in the end, it's very likely that you will eventually need to support and add features to it later on.

Before starting to review code it is imperative that you understand its context. Carefully read the merge request description, check external links and make sure you know what the changed code is supposed to be doing. If the submission does not include enough information for you to gather this context you should request it and only get back to reviewing it after context is provided. It's a common practice to have a checklist template listing the things that should be done or provided while submitting code for review. If your team uses one, check if all steps were correctly followed. As for how to review code, practices vary a lot, for instance, some teams require reviewers to download the submitted code and run it in their own machines to confirm it works as expected, others only expect that peers inspect the code without running it. Even if your team does not require testing the code in your own machine, you should consider doing so in some situations as it will help you gain context about the feature and therefore allow for a better review.

The most important thing to consider when reviewing code is of course the correctness of the solution. Try to think about edge and corner cases, consider data validation, error handling, performance, and security. Ultimately the most important thing is ensuring the experience of the users, but that's not all that matters in a code review. Software is written for other engineers to keep effectively working on it as the system evolves, reviewing how the code is written is also important. Most teams are composed of experienced and less experienced engineers and everyone should be able to work in all parts of the system, so a good reference is asking yourself if junior engineers would be able to easily understand that code. Confirm that the code added is consistent with the patterns and styles defined by the team. It's even better if you use linters and code formatters to automatize that work so people don't even need to think about this. Check for code duplication. Especially in big codebases, it's easy for people to rewrite functionality that already exist somewhere else in the codebase. Don't forget to review tests, make sure they are covering all the major success and failure flows as well as edge cases.

As you go through the code make comments as if you were having an actual conversation with the author. Point out the things you did not understand and ask questions, make suggestions on how to make the code more readable or simpler and propose different ways to implement algorithms. Be humble, before criticizing try to understand why things were done in a certain way, perhaps the author had a different perspective on the problem that you did not consider. The language and tone you use in your comments is important, be empathetic, kind, and suggestive and avoid criticizing directly. Instead, use indirect language such as asking questions that both helps you to better understand decisions but also exposes your ideas. For example, instead of saying "Don't do X," say "Have you considered doing Y? It seems more appropriate than X in this situation." Or, instead of saying "This is not clear," say "How about this other way, I think it would be more straightforward [and provide an example]." Comments are a lot more effective when you provide a reasoning, people are more receptive when they understand the "why." Don't expect everyone to have the same context you have, things that are obvious to you might not be as clear to others. By being explicit you are avoiding an otherwise preventable back and forth conversation. Most people think about merge requests as a place to fix what is wrong but they are also a great opportunity to acknowledge and compliment. Don't spare comments like "This code is neat!" "I love what you did here," "I was not considering this case, great insight!"

Not all review comments need to be addressed or are worth investing time on discussions, some are just personal preferences or stylistic suggestions with a low impact. It's ok to point these out in your review but if you are going to do so, explicitly highlight that in your comment and let the author decide whether they want or not to address the suggestion. If they want to keep things as they are, don't make any other comments about it unless the person explicitly wants to discuss more about it. In these situations, the goal is more about exposing people to different points of view, not necessarily to change their opinion; it's ok if they don't agree with you and decide not to accept the suggestion.

Reviewing code is not just about preventing bugs and keeping the quality of the codebase it's also a great opportunity for sharing knowledge among team members. Use your comments as a medium to teach fellow engineers about parts of the system they might not be aware of, to explain why certain code patterns are better than others and where they can learn more about these topics. Reference internal documentation, share blog posts, recorded talks, and recommend books. Recommending other people in the company who can provide more context is also a great way to promote connections amongst the team. Using async communication during reviews is great because it leaves a track of the discussions and allows other engineers to jump in and participate, but in case the submitted code drifts too far from your expectations or if it would require a complex or long explanation, it might be worth it to break the process and invite the author for a "pair review" session. The idea is to go over the merge request explaining the problems and providing context that would otherwise be too time-consuming to do over text. In this case, it's extra important to be careful with your language and posture, keep the mood light and demonstrate your goal is not to criticize but to align expectations and share information that the author might be unaware of. Under no circumstances use this for unloading your frustrations or use a judgmental tone; if you do this, it's very likely that people will get uncomfortable and defensive, defeating the purpose of the session and making it unproductive. People should feel happy that someone is taking their time to teach them, not anxious.

Code submitted for review is just a few steps from being available for users and therefore generating value to the product. That means it's strategic to the team and to the business to treat them as a priority and get them done as quickly as possible. At the same time, there's no need to drop everything you are doing just because there's a new merge request submission, finish what you are doing and then move on to the review. A good practice is to check open merge requests before starting on new things or when you are coming back from a break, that way you reduce context switching. If you are working on an unusually complex and long task that requires your full attention, consider sharing that with the team and asking other people to step in for you so you don't become a blocker. Keep in mind that delaying code reviews is bad for the team performance as it significantly slows down the development feedback loop, so do your best to prioritize them.

Key takeaways:

- Own the process of code review just like you own the code that you write yourself.

- Before looking at the code, gather the context and goals of the activity you are going to evaluate.

- Go beyond the happy path of the functionality, try to think about what is missing such as edge cases and non-addressed risks.

- Ensure the code is clear and easy to understand, even by less experienced engineers.

- Be empathetic in your comments, prefer suggestions instead of strong statements.

- If expectations drift too far, consider doing a pair review to increase collaboration and get things sorted faster.

2.10 Submitting Your Code for Review

Just like when reviewing other people's code, there are many practices that will help you be more effective when submitting your own code. The overall goal is to make the process fast, so you can deliver value to users; efficient, so problems are captured early on; and easy for teammates to collaborate. Once you have code ready for review, your number one priority should be to get it merged. Although it is OK to start new activities while you wait for teammates to review, try to be responsive to comments and change requests, prioritizing fixing comments as soon as possible. The sooner these are tackled, the earlier you will add value to users.

Prior to asking others to review your code it's important that you review it yourself. While working on a feature you will be immersed in the context of the project trying to fit your changes within existing code. Taking a moment to look at your work in isolation helps to focus and makes it easier to identify problems. Most code collaboration platforms provide a clean interface that highlights which code was added, removed, or changed, so take advantage of these. Read line by line confirming your code will be easy to understand by your teammates, check if names are accurate, and that you are following project conventions. This is also a good moment to review your assignment instructions one last time, double-check if you've completed everything that was specified, look again for corner cases you might have missed and confirm that you've achieved the business goal of the assignment. Review the tests you wrote and if you are satisfied with what is covered. Check if you forgot to add or update code comments, logs, and docs.

Once you are finished with your self review, it's time to think about the experience of the people who are going to review your code. Remember that you are ultimately responsible for the code you ship so when your peers find problems and request changes it means you have the chance of fixing those before they cause problems later on in production. The easier it is for your teammates to review your code, the more effectively they'll do it, increasing the chances of catching issues. Before inviting people to review, write a description, including what the goals of your merge request are, provide context and link to relevant content such as the original assignment document and other relevant assets. Inform if there is any special setup the reviewer needs to do in order to run the code and write down easy to follow instructions. Include a checklist of the things you consider important to be verified. If there's a user interface, take screenshots and attach them or record a small video of the feature being used. An effective practice, especially for more complex merge requests, is to add your own review comments providing more context about the changes you've made, you can also add notes indicating critical parts that should be reviewed more carefully and even explicitly ask for people's opinions on things that you are insecure about in your code.

The amount of code you submit for review matters, the longer it is, the harder it is for reviewers to concentrate and give proper attention to it. Doing a good review is a time-consuming process, so when people encounter a huge wall of code, they will naturally switch to fast glancing through code so they can get it done in a reasonable time for them to get back to their own assignments. As we said before, it's in your interest that reviewers thrive in their work so it's in your best interest that they have a great experience reviewing your code. Each merge request submission ideally has a single objective, if you can't write a title for it that does not have the word "and" in it, it's probably a sign that you are doing too much at once. It's better and a lot easier to review multiple focused merge requests than it's to do a single one that does everything. Another advantage of short submissions is that because they can be reviewed faster, they are less likely to generate code conflicts and when they do, it's usually easier to fix. Getting used to making short and objective merge request submissions is also beneficial to your own flow of development as it will help you to focus on a single problem at a time, reducing context switching, and facilitating your self-review of the code. A good idea is to define a policy on the max size of merge requests and make it a team policy.

It's important that you are critical of your work and demonstrate to your peers that you are open to receiving feedback. If there's something that you are not fully happy about the code you wrote, don't wait for the reviewer to pick it up, add a comment explaining why you decided to do it this way but that you are not fully happy about it, explicitly ask if reviewers can think of a better way to do it. Proactively identify and communicate risks you are aware of, and tell how you are mitigating them but also inform when you don't have full context about something in particular so people with more information can fill in the gaps. When you are not proactive about risks, you are giving the impression that either you don't know about them or that you decided they are not relevant enough; both cases don't speak well about your work. Collaboration is the main goal of having a merge request process, so contrary to what many aim for, it's positive that your team is having discussions before merging new code. As long as people are learning and not constantly repeating the same mistakes it is actually a positive indication of a mature, well-oiled team.

Hopefully, after you submit your code for review, you will receive feedback on things that you should change and questions about your decisions. Regardless of the nature of the comments, it's very important not to take them personally. Remember they are comments about that particular code that you wrote, not about you. As you go through the comments, demonstrate that you are grateful for them, use phrases like "good call, I'll make that change" to encourage more collaboration and build a trusting relationship between you and your teammates. Be empathetic and try to understand from people's perspective why they are making those suggestions. Asking questions instead of counter arguing is a great tool to maintain a friendly tone and at the same time gather more context before presenting your arguments. Very often people will disagree because they each have different assumptions about the problem and the solution, asking questions is very effective in identifying these different perspectives. For example, you can say things like "can you explain a little more why you did not like my proposed solution?" or "I didn't understand your comment, can you please explain it in a different way?" or even "perhaps I'm missing something, can you point to me where I can learn more about your suggestion?" It's OK to push back and counter argue, if you are going to do so, keep a professional tone, present your arguments, provide links to external sources you are leveraging and give examples. At the same time, it's important not to overdo it; after you've made your point, consider if the problem is really worth the time you and your teammates are investing and if there's really a significant gain in either approach. If there isn't just be pragmatic and say something like "I'm not 100% convinced this is the best solution but let's do as you say and perhaps we can reevaluate it sometime in the future" and move on. Knowing when to stop is especially important when arguing with someone hierarchically above you. Do not refrain from presenting your professional opinion, it's actually a great sign of maturity when you do so. But watch for signs that the person has already made their decision or that they don't want to invest more time in that discussion. Remember that there are no winners and losers, everyone in the team is on the same boat working for the success of the product, you are just disagreeing on the path that is going to take you there.

Key takeaways:

- Do a self-review of your own code before you invite others to collaborate.

- Make it easy for your teammates to review your code by writing a detailed description, highlighting key parts and providing screenshots or diagrams.

- Keep your merge requests as short and focused as possible.

- Keep an open mind and demonstrate you are grateful for the feedback you receive.

2.11 Pair Programming

Pair programming is the practice of having two people simultaneously collaborating on the same code. There are variations of the methodology but it usually involves two people switching between the roles of pilot and co-pilot. Despite the role each person plays, they should both communicate throughout the whole time and decide together how to tackle an assignment, but only the pilot is allowed to type while the co-pilot can only review what is written. In most companies, pair programming is used for teaching less experienced engineers on technical and business topics they are not familiar with, unblocking and speeding up the development of a task. While this is certainly a good use case for the practice, there are many other reasons for a team to build a culture of pair programming. When it's used strategically, pair programming is a great tool to continuously promote collaboration and knowledge sharing amongst team members.

Some methodologies such as the Extreme Programming (XP) preach pair programming should be employed full time by engineers. While there are certainly some benefits to this approach, much can be gained from a regular but less intense practice. Some situations where pair programming can be extremely effective are when kickstarting big projects, fixing complex bugs, refactoring, and while working on parts of the system where knowledge is concentrated in a few individuals. These are all situations where collaboration is key to the long-term success of the project. Pair programming is also an excellent tool to increase the sense of ownership amongst the team. When decisions emerge from collective participation, people will naturally feel they have a greater mandate and are more likely to defend and promote these ideas. Another great use for pair programming is during the onboarding of new team members. New hires face a great deal of challenges adapting to a team; having pair programming sessions with different people accelerates their acclimation on the project and helps in building bonds with their new teammates.

Keep in mind that just because you are programming with someone else it does not mean that you are automatically getting the benefits of pair programming. A good session is all about communication; practice explaining what you are doing while you code, explain your decisions and why you chose it over other options. Confirm your pair understands your train of thought and that they are on board with the solution you are proposing. Expect that some people will be less communicative than others and make it your goal to involve and promote participation from them even if this is the case. Explicitly ask questions that stimulate participation and collaboration. By doing so you are creating an open environment and given time, people will start to open up and feel comfortable being more vocal. Be careful not to interrupt as people talk, let them finish their thoughts before you give your opinion. When in the role of co-pilot, avoid being too fast on pointing at mistakes from the person in the pilot role, give them some time to perceive typos and mistakes themselves. Constantly correcting over simple things can be annoying and might come off as pedantic. When you feel it's time to intervene, use a suggestive or propositive tone so it feels like collaboration instead of finger-pointing. Effective pair programming requires a safe environment so it should be carried out with a kind, positive and friendly tone at all times. An excellent way to promote a safe environment is by allowing yourself to be vulnerable, don't be afraid to recognize your mistakes and be honest about what you don't know and about your insecurities, for some people it might be intimidating to pair with an overconfident person.

A key part of the pair programming discipline is switching roles so both people have time as pilot and copilot. Some teams establish a fixed time period for these switches to occur while others do it more freely as the session progresses. As a rule of thumb, the greater the experience gap between the people participating is, the more the person with less experience should be in the role of pilot. Experienced engineers move faster and sometimes they don't identify when it's too accelerated for the other person. By having the less experienced person on the keyboard, everyone is forced to communicate more and it's easier to identify if someone is just mindlessly typing without really understanding what is going on. TDD is especially effective and fun to practice during pair programming sessions. Some teams actually use it to govern the pilot/co-pilot switching dynamic. In this approach, the pilot starts by writing a failing test and roles switch right after so the other person is in charge of typing while the pair works to make the test pass. Once it passes, the same person in the pilot writes a new failing test and the roles are again switched. This flow is repeated until the task is completed.

Although extremely useful and beneficial, pair programming can be exhausting; the need for continuous interaction drains the energy from some people a lot more than it does from others. To make the session less tiring, define a break policy, for instance, you can make five-minute pauses every 30 minutes or every time you make some significant progress. Pausing is not just invigorating but you will notice it actually helps unblocking and solving problems as rested brains are better at solving complex problems.

Effective collaboration is hard, it requires trial and error and a lot of practice and pair programming is one of the more intense forms of collaboration for a software engineer. Coding with another person is challenging as each engineer has their own way of thinking and approaching problems; pair programming requires an active effort from both parties to find a flow that is comfortable for everyone. It's a good practice to periodically ask and give feedback to your peers after pair programming sessions, that way you are creating opportunities for learning about what works best for each person in your team and have the opportunity to learn and correct your own mistakes as well as realign expectations.

Key takeaways:

- There are many benefits from the regular practice of pair programming, from building bonds between team members to sharing knowledge and promoting code ownership.

- Continuous communication is the key for the success of pair programming sessions, always explain your train of thought and justify your decisions.

- Keep an honest communication, don't be afraid to be vulnerable.

- When pairing with a less experienced person, give them more keyboard time.

- Give and ask for feedback so you and your teammates can improve collaboration skills.

2.12 Collaborative Design

Designing software comprehends everything, from defining what the user interface looks like to what architecture and algorithms will be employed to the problem you are working on. There's no absolute right way to build a software component, decisions are always biased by engineers' own experience and the context it's surrounded. Strategic engineers know that making technical decisions involves much more than just comparing the available tools or choosing the fastest algorithm. For example, you might know the perfect tool to solve a problem, if your team is not comfortable working with it, you might be generating more problems than solving. At the very least you will need to consider the cost of training people before committing to it. **Getting the input from teammates and promoting discussions is one of the best ways we have to expand our often nearsighted opinions and let others fill in the gaps by providing other perspectives.** Collaborative software design is all about being humble and working through our personal limitations.

In the *Development Flow* section, we defined that before starting to write software you should plan and validate your solution and that's actually the best moment to promote design collaboration. Once the code is written it's much harder to change things, especially because the cost of building it was already paid, so the decision becomes whether you should release what you have or invest more time on a new solution. The option that delivers value to customers right away will always have a big edge in these situations. Not everything you work on needs more collaboration than the usual pair programming or a merge request process, but there are some signs you can pay attention to identify when to promote other collaborative practices. The amount of code you will need to add or change is often a good indication that you should invite more people to the discussion. That includes big refactorings, changes in architecture, and new product verticals. You should also take into account how often teammates will need to directly or indirectly interact with that piece of code; if it's a central piece that connects with a lot of other parts and that will need continuous maintenance and improvement, more people should have a say on how it should be designed. The amount of options you will need to evaluate before picking a solution is also a good indicator of the need to provide more visibility on your decision-making process. It's also good that you trust your intuition. If you are not fully happy with the solutions you've come up with or you feel that there are edge cases you might not have considered, that's also a sign to promote more collaboration. In all of these cases, what you are ultimately doing is evaluating risk; the higher the risk your work represents to the codebase or to the product, the higher is the need to involve more people in the discussion.

Debating code design is one of those things that work especially well when done asynchronously through text documents. Explaining software architecture is particularly hard to do if you don't provide code samples or let people take their time to analyze the existing context of the changes you are proposing. In software teams, this kind of document to discuss decisions is usually called a Request For Comments (RFC). RFCs were originally created by the Internet Engineering Task Force (IETF), which is the organization responsible for defining Internet standards; naturally, they also standardized the format of the document people should submit their proposals. RFCs were later adopted by open source projects and have made their way into the corporate world. The goal of an RFC is not to document what will be the final solution but rather to propose an approach and have it scrutinized by peers. In the corporate world, there's less need for the formality of the IETF standards so teams mix and match what makes sense for their context; commonly, an RFC document would have at least the following sections: "Title," "Context and scope," "Goals and non-goals," "Proposal (the main body)," and "Alternatives considered." It's pretty easy to find templates online that you can adapt to your team's context. After writing the document, publish it in a place where it's easy for your teammates to make comments and propose changes.

While you should always start by publishing a text document, it's not reasonable to expect that's the end of your work. Perhaps on a very mature team people will naturally start flocking in and posting their comments, but that won't be the usual experience for most people. After posting your RFC you should make an active effort to bring people into the discussion, so make sure you inform the team about it on a public channel. If there are specific people with a lot of context on the topic you are proposing, send them a direct message asking for their contribution. Use team meetings to inform about the RFC and invite people to review the document and participate in the discussion. You can also use these synchronous moments to settle some specific points where the asynchronous process is prolonging more than you wish. Scheduling a meeting to debate an RFC when people haven't yet reviewed the document is usually not productive. Either discussions will take longer because people will need to acquire context before participating or they won't properly collaborate and just accept whatever was proposed. Prefer promoting async discussions and use meetings strategically only to decide on the things where arguments are not converging.

RFCs are for people in all career levels; junior and senior engineers should engage in the practice of publishing proposals and making comments on other people's documents. To develop a collaborative team where people are propositive and critical of each other's work as well as their own work, always encourage the participation of less experienced engineers in RFCs. Besides learning from being exposed to new technical contexts and practicing their collaboration skills, they will often bring in fresh ideas and will help identify decisions that are poorly described or too complex; in both situations, this is good input for you to adapt your document or rethink your solution. When responding to comments, use the same principles you'd use for a merge request, making people feel comfortable and welcome to keep ideas coming. Promoting collective ownership is yet another benefit of RFCs. Allowing everyone to give their opinions, identifying risks and suggesting different approaches should build a sense that the whole team is responsible for the evolution of the codebase. The idea of "my code" or "my architecture" should not exist. In a mature team, people should own every part of the project, a collective decision means everyone celebrates success when things go well and everyone is accountable for mistakes and for fixing things when they go wrong.

Key takeaways:

- Promote design collaboration early on before you start writing the code so it's cheap to change.

- The frequency people will need to interact with that piece of software and the amount of code it will need are good signs that more people should have a say on how the code should be designed.

- Prefer discussing over text documents where people have more time to reflect on your proposed architecture and form their opinions, RFCs are a great format for that.

- Don't wait for people to join in the discussions, actively invite them to participate, including the less experienced teammates.

2.13 Documentation

Especially in small teams, documentation is often left behind as a non-priority, which is very controversial because if you ask, most engineers will recognize it as important and will probably say that they should be investing more on docs. But, on the day-to-day when pressure from stakeholders is on and fires are popping in, most will just leave docs to another time when things are calmer, which, surprise! surprise! never happens. That behavior generates the natural tendency of docs only being prioritized, if ever, when it's already too late and the lack of docs is directly impacting team performance. Strategic engineers treat docs as part of their work routine; just like tests, they are an integral part of the process of developing features and fixing bugs. It's a work that costs very little if done gradually and pays off in the long run. It's also one of those things that doesn't fully work if there's only one person in the team doing it, so your goals should be to build a culture where everyone is active and owns docs, just like everyone owns the codebase.

Writing good documentation is no trivial task; the first problem is that there are many types of documentation that apply to different contexts, and what is considered a good practice in some situations might not apply to another. There's also the issue of considering the size of your company, how often you are onboarding new people and what is the level of these people joining the organization. Business context also matters, if you are working on a product for law firms, it's safe to expect most engineers won't have training in that domain so perhaps you should be writing more documentation. Evaluating risk is another important factor that should be taken into account. No organization should rely on key knowledge stored in a few engineer's heads, so it's necessary to consider what will happen if people change jobs, go on vacation, or are for any reason unable to work. Lastly, team members, as co-owners of the documentation process, should have a say on what they want to be in their docs and how it should be written. It's positive that this is an evolving practice that adapts as the project grows, as long as it's being periodically debated and evaluated it's likely that you are on the right track.

Besides the benefits for the team, **writing docs is an excellent exercise to help organize ideas and consolidate knowledge.** Writing docs has a similar effect as pair programming in the sense that it forces you to think about things and express them in a way that is convincing and easy to understand. It will help you identify gaps in your solutions and be more confident about your work. Equally, being able to write about your work in a simple way is a sign that teammates will also find it easy to understand it. The process of writing docs is also another potential point of validation and alignment. You can send drafts of your work for review to teammates so you can gather feedback to improve your writing but at the same time, also have people reviewing the technical content of it.

Docs are only useful if people are reading them, there's no point in documenting things that will be left in a dark corner and that gets remembered once a year when someone notices they are outdated and useless. Documentation should be stored somewhere where it's easy for people to find, ideally some place people are frequently interacting with. It's also important that the tool you use to store docs allows searching, so it's easy to find things when they are needed. Docs are a living organism, they need to evolve and adapt as the business and the technology changes. When deciding about what to document, it's important to ponder about maintenance. Outdated docs serve no purpose and can even lead to communication and technical issues. It's a known fact that it's hard to keep docs up-to-date, so the rule of thumb is, if it changes too often, it's going to require a lot of effort to keep it up-to-date; in that case, if docs are not critical to the operation of the product it's likely that you'd be better off without them and just require people to look at the code or talk to peers. For the sake of maintenance, different types of docs should be stored in different places, the closer they are to the subject they address, the higher are the chances of people finding them when they need and that they will remember to update when there are changes.

As shown in the *Development flow* section, docs should be part of your workflow as an engineer, they should not be a separate task from the process of programming. The best moment to update docs is when you are working on the things they describe, the second best moment is while you are reading them and find issues or missing information. When writing documentation, think about the situations where it's going to be consumed and who is its primary consumer. That will help you decide how long the text should be, how deep you should go, and how it should be formatted. Consider how much context you need to provide for the reader to understand the information. Provide working code samples that can be copied and pasted so people can quickly test things and use it as a building block to adapt to their specific needs. Include external links that complement the information in case someone needs more context, or perhaps if it's a complex problem that's been well covered in a book or a blog post, providing that reference can save you the time to write the content from scratch. If something is worth being documented, it's usually a good sign that it's of people's interest so always consider if you should provide visibility to the team about what you added or changed. Even if it's not useful right away, just knowing that piece of information is documented enables people to search for it when they need it later. In addition, that kind of visibility serves the purpose of allowing more people to review your work and provide feedback, and is also a good way to refresh people's mind about parts of the system they haven't worked on lately or ever. This generates a flow where there's always someone sharing knowledge about different topics and increasing everyone's knowledge about the system. As the product changes, you write and update: code, automated tests, and docs; everything is bundled and part of your job as a software engineer.

Text is not the only way to document, video can also be used as a form of documentation. For instance, suppose you know a lot about a part of the system that a new hire is going to work on. Instead of writing a documentation or even scheduling a meeting to explain how it works, you can record a video and send it to the whole team so other people interested in the subject can also watch in their own time. Using video as your main source of documentation is probably not advisable in most cases. It might work for some high level business or product overview and core concepts, but other than that, it's likely that it will get outdated quickly and, unlike written documentation, it's costly to produce and update video. There are other problems with it, such as making it harder to search information, and not allowing people to quickly scan over it to check if it contains what they need.

Now that we've gone through many of the core concepts and considerations on documentation, we can get a bit more practical and apply what we discussed to some of the most common scenarios and opportunities where docs can be used.

Documenting Code

Code documentation, especially in the form of code comments, is one of those endless discussions among software engineers. Many will say that code should be self-documented in the sense that, if it's not possible to understand something just by reading the code it means that the code is poorly written so it should be refactored to something that is more comprehensible. While the vast majority of engineers will agree about the importance of writing easy to understand code, it's reasonable to consider that some problems are intrinsically complicated such that it is beneficial to provide extra context in the form of code comments. More important than picking a side in this argument is to understand the motivations behind both approaches and use in your favor. When you feel the need to write comments in order to make your solution more understandable, use this feeling as an indication that you should invest a little more time trying to improve your code. Consider inviting a teammate for a quick pair programming session to see if they can propose a better solution or have an insight to improve it. The key is not stressing out and knowing when to stop, if you can't come up with something simpler, just add code comments and move on.

When writing code comments, focus on making explicit why things were written in such a way instead of saying what the code is doing or how it's doing it. Most times, by using good variable and method names, it's possible to write code that clearly tells what it does. But explaining why certain approach was chosen instead of some other or justifying why it was necessary to employ some unusual construction it's often not possible to do just through the code. In all situations, be critical of your work and use your judgment to spot what can be refactored to a clearer form and what could benefit from comments.

Also in this category are "doc strings" which are code comments that usually follow a standardized format to document classes, methods, and their parameters. Standards will vary depending on which programming language you are using but the key advantage of this type of code comment is that they enable tools like code editors to pick up more information and assist other engineers using that code. It's also common and encouraged to provide usage examples in the doc strings.

Documenting Interfaces

Whenever there's communication between two or more systems or parts of the code, there's an interface, be it explicit or not. Interfaces define boundaries and are extremely important not only for organizing code but also to reduce cognitive load, they abstract complex things through smaller (and ideally simple) facades, freeing your mind to focus on building new things while enjoying the use of an abstracted service. While interfaces built for usage within the same team often don't require a lot of documentation, the further the distance between who defines the interface and who consumes it, the greater is the need for more and better documentation.

When building an API to be consumed by another team within your organization, it's a good idea to document the available endpoints, the parameters, and what the responses look like. In fact that kind of documentation can be written even before you start writing the software that implements it. Interface documentation can be used as an alignment tool for teams to discuss their needs and restrictions without the cost of rebuilding software multiple times until a final design is reached. Once settled on an initial version, both teams can start working each on their side of the project basing their decisions on an agreed interface. That way, the team providing the API will build their service from the documentation blueprint being confident they are on the path to provide the right functionality and the team consuming the API can also work on their side by simulating the expected behavior while it's not ready for use. Of course that doesn't mean there won't be changes along the way, but it's a very effective way to start and promote the changes as they are needed; if planning was well done, hopefully they will be small and easy for both teams to adapt.

Building docs for a public facing API requires a lot more attention and effort and they can make a big difference on the success of a product. Integrating systems is a complex task but good documentation can take a lot of the pain out of the work. When writing docs, you must take into account that people reading it will have very different levels of context with regard to the business you are providing and different levels of experience with programming. Provide as much information as you can and carefully describe parameters and behavior, especially the ones that involve risky operations. Good docs can save money and time by reducing the need for customer support and they are usually a cost-effective investment because public APIs are not meant to change often so they need less maintenance. Besides the textual information you are going to write, consider the user experience of the people reading your docs. Consider breaking the document into sections providing a quick start guide and examples on how to use each endpoint. Also think about the layout of the page, is it easy to follow? Is it easy to search for information? Avoid building documentation pages from scratch, there are many templates specifically designed for hosting documentation; pick one and customize it to your needs. Consider using standards like Swagger/OpenAPI to document HTTP APIs, these are widely adopted by the software development community and have an ecosystem of tools that support them. For instance, there are tools to automatically generate a web page from these specs for you to publish online. Other tools can help developers writing code to integrate with your API by providing contextual information and validation as they write the code.

Documenting the Repository

The industry standard for documenting code repositories is having a file called README at the root folder. This file should have all the basic information needed for someone to run the project without external help. It usually starts with a brief description of what is the project followed by a quick-start or setup guide that includes external dependencies and installation instructions. It's also common to provide information about the main features and operational commands such as how to write tests or to make advanced configuration. Another good idea is to include a section with known issues that can happen during installation and usage along with instructions on how to fix them. Long documentation usually includes an index at the top for quick accessing sections but it's not uncommon to break it into multiple files and reference them from the README.

Documenting Architecture

Architecture is a broad term in software engineering, it can refer to things like how to organize code in files, how to compose classes, definitions on how different applications interact with each other in an organization as well as the many in between concepts. Documenting architecture is usually something that shouldn't happen too early in the project's lifecycle. There is too much volatility in that initial phases and there's a lot to be tested, learned and consolidated. It's probably better to let things settle down before investing on documenting architecture. Conversely, as the project and the team grows so does the need to write clear guidelines on it.

The best place to store architecture docs will depend on team dynamics and people's preference. Some teams will keep them in the README file, others will have a separate document or repository and some will move it away to a wiki or some form of shared file system. There's no right or wrong. It all depends on the current stage of the project and people's preferences. As long as it's easy to search and find things and people incorporate the tool in their routine, consulting and updating docs as the system evolves, it should be fine. Diagrams are an excellent visualization tool and should be encouraged in architecture docs, so it's a good idea to pick a tool where it's easy to save and display images. At the same time, images are hard to version and to update, so it's even better if you can use a tool that converts text to diagrams such as Mermaid.JS.

There are some established frameworks for writing architecture docs; one of the most popular ones is the C4 model so consider adapting it or incorporating some of its ideas; writing good architecture docs is not easy and people have invested a great deal of time thinking and testing what works best and what doesn't, so there's no need for you to reinvent the wheel.

Another approach to architecture documentation leverages the fact that architecture is dynamic and always changing, so instead of having a single document with the consolidated state of the system, it embraces that changing nature by tracking the history of evolution of the architecture, much like Git commits tells the history of the evolution of the code. One popular model that adopts this is called Architecture Decision Records (ADRs). ADRs are immutable documents that detail things such as date, context, considered options, risks, and decisions on changes made to the architecture of the project. They are useful not only to understand what is the state of the system but to allow looking back and understanding why decisions were made in the past. They are also very effective for communicating these changes to the team because they are shorter and focused on just what changed from the previous standard. "Consolidated" and "diff" approaches for architecture documentation are not conflicting and they can both be employed for different situations in a single project.

Documenting Operation

Software projects are unique, each one is composed of a wide variety of frameworks, external libraries, practices, tools, and a specific context and business goals. Just knowing the tech stack is usually not enough for one to be able to operate a minimally complex project. Mature projects need an instructions manual with information about how to run and perform routine operations such as running tests, deploying, executing custom commands, and fixing common problems. One might think that this kind of documentation is only useful for new people joining the team but it's actually very important for everyone, especially when a team is maintaining many different projects. Nobody should be required to memorize how to do everything in a project, this is an anti-pattern, and a very unproductive one.

An especially important use for this kind of documentation is for incident management. Ideally, the most probable ways the software can break are already mapped and the steps to fix them are available for use during a crisis situation. For web applications, some of the very basic things to have documented is how to restore the database from a backup and how to restart servers. Don't assume that this is trivial or that senior engineers will know how to do it, you have to account for the unique characteristics of each project and the pressure that builds during a crisis situation. Following clear instructions is much faster and safer than having people trying to remember every step and command they need to run. The process of writing this documentation is also important as you will often learn that some things don't work as you expected and have the chance to fix them before they are needed in a critical situation, no one wants to be debugging commands while the system is down. Brainstorm with your team to gather what are the most important cases that you should be prepared for and write guides on how to fix them.

It's very easy for operation docs to get outdated so your team should nurture a culture of updating them whenever someone bumps into a problem. For the most critical pieces, such as the incident management guides, it's important to periodically revisit them from time to time and execute the steps to confirm that it is still working as expected.

Frequently Asked Questions (FAQ)

Frequently Asked Questions (FAQ) documents are a great form of documentation. Usually the goal of FAQs is not to provide detailed answers to questions but rather to provide a short summary on a topic. Each team can decide how they want their FAQ document to be structured, but it's probably a good idea to keep answers short and provide a link that addresses the issue in full detail in case someone needs more information. You can bootstrap a FAQ document by brainstorming a few questions you imagine a person joining the team would ask. This is a great way to get things going, but the goal should be to keep feeding the document as the project evolves. To identify what else should go in the FAQ, you can make it a personal or team rule to never answer the same question twice, if that happens, you are not allowed to write the answer again, you must add it to the FAQ and send the link to the person who asked it. Be careful as not to appear arrogant or intimidating when sending the link with the answer, explain to the person that it's a relevant question that other people might have as well so it's a nice one to be featured in the FAQ.

2.14 Remove Toil

Any repetitive activity required for the proper functioning of the system or to the process of building the system and that requires manual intervention from a human being can be considered toil work. As systems grow, activities that used to require little effort start to need more intervention; commonly, this happens gradually and it's easy to go unnoticed how much time ends up going down the drain. **Engineers need to constantly evaluate the use of their time in order to identify when it's strategic to invest on solutions that remove toil work.** To make that decision you need to balance risk, cost of operation of the current setup, cost of building a new solution, and cost of maintaining the new solution. Identifying the right moment to act is also important; if it's too early, you might not have the full context, risking your solution not addressing the actual problem. Or you might overestimate the future cost of the toil work and end up with a solution that is more complex than what you needed and in some cases that is more costly to build and maintain than the original problem.

For an engineer, the most obvious solution to overcome toil work is automation. There are many levels of automation, for example, if you have to periodically clean up some database tables, at first it might be good enough to just open the database administration interface and click to delete the lines that shouldn't be there; after some time, you get tired of clicking and write a script that you can run from the terminal, further on you might add a button to run the script with a single click, finally you can set up a periodic cron job to fully automate the work removing the need of any manual intervention. That kind of gradual progression is very common to happen and is a good example on how to remove toil work avoiding overengineering (we will talk more about overengineering in the next chapter). At the same time it's important to beware that automation comes with a cost. In the previous example, the activity of cleaning up the database might be a crucial one for the smooth functioning of the system, so while it's certainly better not to depend on a human for it to happen, the natural tendency for something that gets automated is for us to forget about it. There's a reasonable chance that the automation will eventually break due to any kind of unforeseen change and you will only notice the failure when it causes an incident. In that case, the solution might be to add some monitoring that can alert you as soon as it breaks. Notice how fixing the initial problem leads to more software to maintain (both the script and the monitoring tool); make sure you understand the trade-offs so the net result is positive.

Customer support is frequently a great toil work accumulator and deserves special attention. In the rush to get problems fixed and customers happy, it's easy to just do whatever is quicker at the moment and not look at the big picture. While on support duty, observe what are the issues and requests that are constantly showing up. Often when looking at one individual task, it's not worth the effort to build a robust solution, but when observing the aggregated time spent on similar tasks, the upside becomes clear. Repeating support tasks are also good indicators of missing features in the product so consider if the best solution is to automate the work of engineers in support or to go the extra mile and invest in a user facing feature and eliminate the need for people to get in contact with support altogether.

Complexity is another source of toil that is often overlooked. Complexity can be categorized as essential or accidental. Essential complexity is good complexity, it is the type that is related to the domain of the problem you are working on and it is required to deliver value to users. Conversely, accidental complexity is bad complexity, it's caused by bad architecture and intentional and unintentional decisions that could be avoided or fixed with no loss to engineers or users of the product.

In one of Vinta's projects we had a critical part of the system depending on an unreliable external integration that ran once per day. Because this integration would fail from time to time the team created processes to manually check if things were properly executed for the day. As the product grew and more features were built around this integration, they naturally started investing more time ensuring everything ran as expected. The situation got worse to the point where we noticed that we were almost dedicating the whole day of a full-time engineer just to monitor this integration and fix issues. Instead of investing time to improve the system to automatically deal with the problematic integration we were continuously in damage contention mode. To counteract the situation we formulated a new plan: we would have two engineers working as a dedicated squad for this integration. That way, even if one of them needed to spend their whole time fixing problems to ensure the execution for the day, the other would still be able to keep working on automation and making the system more resilient to self-recovery from failure. Within a few months of work, the results of these actions were crystal clear. Where it would sometimes take until the end of the day to finish processing the data, the system was now finishing everything automatically before the first engineer started working. This is a great example on how accidental complexity can start as a minor inconvenience and slowly work its way into unproductive use of engineers' time.

Leaky abstractions are a kind of accidental complexity, they happen when parts of the code, especially complex ones, require too much context, or understanding of its internals to be used. For example, suppose your project has an integration with an external service but whenever you want to call an endpoint from their API you need to deal with the process of authenticating the request. Authenticating a request is a repetitive process that often requires understanding of complex protocols and that changes for each service provider. The people responsible for building the integration must know about those but there's no need for every engineer that will use the integration to know about these details. They should be able to just call a method that gives them the information they need. This kind of problem might not be as clear for small teams, but as the codebase and the team grows it becomes more noticeable. There's a moment where it's not possible to have everyone keeping up with every part of the system, so it makes a huge difference to have concealed interfaces that abstract unneeded complexity away from the people consuming it.

Every line of code you write or piece of infrastructure you add increases the load of maintaining the system. Products with a lean mindset need to focus on the things that bring direct value to their clients. While having a database is essential for most products, provisioning, configuring, and maintaining the database infrastructure is a time-consuming activity that has no direct impact on clients [as long as it's working as expected] so it's probably a good idea to pay a little extra to delegate that work to someone else by using a managed solution and use your time to build features. If you are working on a small team, use off-the-shelf tools such as open-source libraries and managed infrastructure whenever possible. As the product grows you can gradually evaluate financial costs and decide whether it's more advantageous to switch to in-house solutions or to stay with the more expensive managed tools.

Engineers should constantly be looking for ways to make their work more efficient by avoiding spending time on non-strategic activities and evaluating costs and trade-offs between alternative approaches and solutions. The benefits of this mindset go beyond business and financial achievements, it promotes a more stimulating and enjoyable work and career.

Key takeaways:

- Toil work naturally builds up as the product and team grows.

- Automate things to a level that is compatible with your current context, but keep in mind that there's also cost to every line of code you add.

- Code complexity can also be considered toil so create abstractions to simplify the use of common tools.

- If possible, prefer off-the-shelf tools and managed infrastructure so you can focus on work that adds direct value to users.

2.15 Tooling

A software engineer, like a craftsperson, should master and leverage the use of tools to design and produce their best work. In some cases, it's possible to deliver great work using tools that are in bad condition or that are not the ideal ones for that particular job, but it surely takes a lot more time and effort than having a toolset that is not only appropriate but well cared for. A knife with a dull blade can deliver a meal that is just as tasteful as one prepared with a sharp blade. Using the right tool is not just about speed, it's also about consistency. **Engineers need to deliver good software over and over throughout multiple years of their career; mistakes are going to happen due to lack of knowledge or accidents, but using the right tools can help you avoid many of them.**

Text editors and IDEs are the source of heated debates among engineers and that's kind of understandable given how much of our time is spent reading code, typing, and searching for things. But the reality is that there's no single better tool for writing code; it will always depend on what programming languages you are using, your personal preferences, the company you are working for, and what tools your teammates are using. Pragmatically speaking, the criteria to pick a programming environment should have the following order of precedence: the one that is officially supported by the company you work for, the one that is most popular among your team members, the one you are most comfortable with, and lastly, the one that is most popular among the community of the programming language you are using. If there's an officially supported IDE in your company, it probably means that there are recommended configurations and plugins that will assist your work in that particular context and these will surely help you to get up to speed faster. If there's no official programming environment, then it's probably better to use whatever your teammates are using. More important than using the best editor is having other people to support you when things break and to point out configurations and tools they've been using to improve their performance. If there's no consensus among the team and each person is using their preferred tool, do the same and use one that you are already comfortable with. If none of the previous is true and you are switching to a new context, such as a new stack, just pick whatever the community is using so you can benefit from the tools that are already available to that ecosystem. After you've picked an editor, it's often worthwhile to learn your way around, how to configure preferences, how to effectively search, what are the most useful and popular plugins, and what shortcuts are worth memorizing. The point is: there's no need to get obsessed, be pragmatic and choose the tool that is more likely to guide you to writing good software.

More important than code editors are the tools that automatically ensure code standards regardless of how team members configure their personal environment. Continuous Integration (CI) tools can be configured to run verifications at every step of the development process, such as on new merge requests or before deployments. If it needs to be enforced, it should be verified on the CI. The rule of thumb is to never trust people's personal environment, the main source of truth is the CI; when someone makes a mistake, the CI should automatically prevent that code from being integrated into the main codebase. CI tools can be configured to run automated tests, ensure test coverage, make security verifications, check for spelling and grammar errors, verifying code styling and linting, and much more. Mature software development teams assume everyone, regardless of how much experience they have, is prone to making mistakes so they leverage the use of CI to enforce their standards and to collectively increase the consistency of the codebase and consequently the experience of the people using the software.

As of the writing of this book, using artificial intelligence to write code is growing in popularity among software engineers. These tools use publicly available software to build a knowledge base that can automatically generate code from a human language specification or by picking up context from your project's code. Provided that such tools are legal in the jurisdiction your company operates and that you are allowed by your company to use them, you should consider incorporating them in your development process. When doing so, always keep in mind that you are ultimately responsible for the code and the consequences of it in your project so don't blindly accept whatever AI generates, double-check everything and test if the code is actually doing what you expect it to do.

It goes without saying that you should always improve the tools you use to work, both by upgrading the ones you already have and by looking for new ones. Just like your computer gets slow every few years and needs an upgrade, you also need to keep evolving the toolset you use for software development. Read release announcements about the products you use to find out about new features that can make your life easier. Research and try new tools that can make you more productive, and check if you can optimize the tools you are already using. In one of Vinta's projects, we had an extensive test suite that grew over time to the point where the CI pipeline was taking more than one hour to run. Not only that, but we also had a few flaky tests that would make the suite fail randomly, further degrading the development experience. We decided that this was no longer reasonable and invested time parallelizing the test suite, making optimizations in the tools and fixing the flaky tests. With relatively low effort we were able to reduce the CI time to five minutes. The gains in team satisfaction even superseded the productivity and financial gains that were already quite significant.

Lastly, don't overlook your health and invest in a comfortable workspace (especially if you work from home). Engineers spend a considerable amount of their day sitting in front of a screen. Use a table and a chair that is adequate to your height (and keep a good body posture). If possible, use an ergonomic keyboard and mouse (and remember to stretch every once in a while). If you are on a remote team, invest in a good headphone and microphone set, it will help to make communication more effective both when you're listening to others and when you are getting your point across. Consider learning touch typing. Touch typing is a technique that allows you to use the keyboard without looking at it and with minimal wrist movement, it is a very fast typing technique and it can prevent diseases such as repetitive strain injury (RSI). It's easy to find touch typing training tools online that teach the concepts and help you practice, it takes some time to get used to but it's definitely worth the investment.

Key takeaways:

- Care for and specialize in your work tools just like a carpenter does for their saw blades, hammers, and nails.

- Use whatever will make you more productive, but prefer tools that are officially maintained and supported by your company so you benefit from built in guardrails.

- Leverage the CI tool as the main source of truth so problems are caught regardless of people's personal development setup.

- If you are allowed, consider using AI code assistants, but keep in mind that you are ultimately responsible for the code you push.

- Invest in your workspace, a good chair makes all the difference and so does having a good headset if you are frequently making video calls.

2.16 References and Further Reading

- "The Future of Programming" by Robert Martin https://www.youtube.com/watch?v=ecIWPzGEbFc

- "Basal Cost of software" by Eduardo Ferro https://www.eferro.net/2021/02/basal-cost-of-software.html

- "TDD is Not Magic" by J. B. Rainsberger https://blog.jbrains.ca/permalink/tdd-is-not-magic

- "TDD Should be Fun" by James Sinclair https://jrsinclair.com/articles/2016/tdd-should-be-fun/

- "The flat success path" by Filipe Ximenes https://www.vintasoftware.com/blog/flat-success-path

- "Quickly improve code readability with Proximity Refactorings" by Nicolas Carlo https://understandlegacycode.com/blog/quickly-improve-code-readability-with-proximity-refactoring/

- "Don't make Clean Code harder to maintain,
  use the Rule of Three" by Nicolas Carlo `https://`
  `understandlegacycode.com/blog/refactoring-rule-`
  `of-three/`

- "The Four Elements of Simple Design" by
  J. B. Rainsberger `https://blog.jbrains.ca/`
  `permalink/the-four-elements-of-simpledesign`

- Google's eng-practices repository `https://google.`
  `github.io/eng-practices/`

- "How to build an effective code review process for
  your team" by Rahim Mitha `https://leaddev.com/`
  `software-quality/how-build-effective-code-`
  `review-process-your-team`

- "Don't rely on memory: knowledge management for
  engineering teams" by Hugo Bessa `https://www.`
  `vintasoftware.com/blog/dont-rely-on-memory-`
  `knowledge-management-for-engineering-teams`

- "Engineering Planning with RFCs, Design Documents
  and ADRs" by Gergely Orosz `https://newsletter.`
  `pragmaticengineer.com/p/rfcs-and-design-docs`

- "What You Need to Know About Your Documentation"
  by Daniele Procida `https://www.youtube.com/`
  `watch?v=qC1OYK5oqDo`

- "Writing docs well: why should a software
  engineer care?" by Lorin Hochstein `https://`
  `surfingcomplexity.blog/2022/11/24/writing-docs-`
  `well-why-should-a-software-engineer-care/`

- "Pockets of rest enable careers" by Will Larson
  `https://lethain.com/pockets-of-rest/`

CHAPTER 3

Risk Management

F. Ximenes, *Strategic Software Engineering*, https://doi.org/10.1007/979-8-8688-0995-8_3

Risk is part of life, there's no escaping from it; every decision we make is consciously or unconsciously imbued with some level of risk management. At work, just by picking one activity over another we are already managing risk. It might be the risk of losing market share to competitors due to a delayed feature, the risk of making customers unhappy due to a postponed bug fix or the risk of having an incident due to a feature that is performing poorly. **Risk management is being conscious about the intrinsic risk of things and leveraging that information to make strategic decisions.** The concept of risk management is quite simple and easy to understand, what is much more complex is measuring it so it's possible to objectively make decisions.

One simple way of quantifying the risk of a certain event is to multiply the likelihood (or frequency) of that event happening by the impact it generates in case it happens (or its criticality). Evaluating the risk of things that are either very likely to happen or that are very impactful is usually quite easy. It's obvious these are the events that we need to be prepared for. What is much harder is prioritizing the things that are not in these extremes, especially in the context where you are juggling between demands from multiple stakeholders and have competitors and customers pushing you to deliver quickly and move on to the next thing.

In an ideal world, everybody has all the time to work on every single edge case and optimize algorithms to be performant for every possible scenario, in practice this is far from reality. In fact, choosing which risks are going to be prioritized is a huge competitive advantage for a team working on a product. So is deciding which are the things that are going to be delayed even though it's known that they might cause the system to break. Making decisions inherently requires taking risks. In practice this means things like letting known issues slip by, accepting an imperfect version of the product in order to deliver faster and building solutions that don't scale at first. That principle applies from high level things such as deciding what's the next feature to ship to very low level such as choosing variable names in the code. Strategic engineers consciously balance their own experience, the business context, and technical factors to evaluate risk and make their decisions.

An important insight on risk management is that most of the time we will be fighting to reduce risks, not to completely remove them. There are many reasons for that, sometimes it is because it's just impossible to completely remove risk but often it is because it's just inefficient to do so, the costs don't justify the benefits. Throughout this chapter, we will be talking about how strategic engineers identify risks, evaluate criticality, balance trade-offs, and use tools, techniques and communication to build better software.

3.1 Own Risk Management

Since there's risk in everything we do, risk management cannot be a job only for the leadership, everyone in the team needs to own it and actively contribute to it. Planning your activities before starting to execute them is one of the most important things you can do in order to manage risk. During planning, reflect on how things can break, look potential blockers, and what can take longer than people expect to build. Of course many issues are not predictable and you will only learn about them in the execution phase, but trying to identify them early on is significantly cheaper. Once you start writing code you've already committed to a certain approach to the problem and rewriting things takes a lot longer than replanning them.

When planning, consider the worst case scenarios, really try to break your assumptions and brainstorm different scenarios. But once you are ready to start crafting a solution, evaluate what is the practical risk of these scenarios occurring and the cost of mitigating them so you can properly decide what actually deserves investment. Taking risks is good and is an expected part of an engineer's job, but it becomes a problem if it's not properly shared with your team. Align with stakeholders your decisions and make sure they are on board with the risks you are taking, be explicit about what are your assumptions and why you think yours is the best approach. Inform how things will break in case assumptions prove incorrect. **It shouldn't be a problem when things break due to a known and planned risk, the failure doesn't change the fact that you took the best decision with the information you had at the time.**

After finishing your work, don't throw away everything you've brainstormed in the planning process, explicitly communicate to your team through code comments, docs, and meetings the risks that are not covered in your solution. It's very important that this is kept in a place where it's easy for teammates to consume and that is likely for them to stumble upon when they are going to integrate or work on that part of the code. The goal is to keep people aware of the conditions where your solution will and will not work and the risks involved. Often the best place for this is right along the code in the form of comments, but as we discussed in the *Documentation* section, writing an Architecture Decision Record (ADR) can also be a great way to consolidate this kind of information.

Don't be afraid to give bad news, the earlier people know about the problems, the earlier everyone can act to mitigate them. Trying to hide or delay information adds negatively to your response performance, it impacts how people perceive your judgment and risk management skills and makes you look irresponsible and reckless. **Worse than seeing an iceberg coming toward you is not saying anything because you are embarrassed you didn't see it earlier.** By being proactive you can sometimes turn a negative perception into a positive one even when the issue was caused by your actions. Consider how you want to communicate depending on the situation, for things that look absolutely critical it might be a good idea to broadcast the problem to the whole team even before you confirm it's actually a problem. If it doesn't look that important, perhaps you should do your own investigation before sounding the alarms. Constantly grabbing everyone's attention to non-critical problems means more context switching and stress for your teammates. In some situations, it will be better to first communicate to your direct leadership to confirm the criticality and importance of the issue before passing it on to the team. In the end, the decision on how to communicate should take into account the impact to the product and the noise to the team. But as a rule of thumb, if you are in doubt, it's better to overcommunicate than to risk something critical slipping by.

Risk management is an integral part of the job of an engineer and it's not just about things breaking. While working on any activity you should be attentive in order to inform your leadership early on if it will take more time than you initially planned. This enables the team to react fast, adapt accordingly, and mitigate the risk of this delay snowballing. Another example is writing a proof of concept before committing to a final solution; by doing that, you are ensuring your solution actually works and mitigating the risk of spending too much time on a dead-end. The same applies to validating assumptions and clearing decisions with stakeholders instead of guessing and risk working on the wrong things.

Strategic engineers know that every decision is ingrained with risk and are consciously thinking about which are worth mitigating and which are not, depending on the current context and future plans for the project. They also own risk management beyond the scope of their job title. Your goal is to make the product as a whole successful, so every time you notice something that doesn't seem right or simply breaks your expectations, you should raise your hand and communicate. That goes for all company areas such as business, design, infrastructure, and even to projects from other teams.

It's also important to keep in mind that people in leadership roles are not superhumans; they are not all-knowing and are prone to making mistakes and forgetting things; the same goes to everyone else in your team. Never assume that because something is done in a certain way it means it must be the best solution; whenever you see documentation or code that looks strange or seems overcomplicated, ask questions and propose other solutions. That kind of attitude will often reveal unknown problems and even when it doesn't, it is usually a great way to identify opportunities for refactoring or to improve documentation. Collaborating with teammates is also a way to mitigate risk. Offer help when you see someone having trouble with their work. Ask questions and make suggestions when analyzing documents, reviewing code, and during team meetings. It's impossible to make software that is 100% fail-proof, but when everyone is constantly alert about each other's work, risk management becomes a lot more effective, which translates into reliable products and effective teams.

Key takeaways:

- Evaluate worst case scenarios when planning your solutions but ponder the trade-offs to decide what is actually worth mitigating.

- Consciously taking risks is a good thing as long as it's communicated and acknowledged by stakeholders.

- Risk management is not just about the things that can break, just by communicating the progress of your work you are helping managers to mitigate business risks.

- Making the product successful is everyone's job so don't be afraid to report the risks you identify in areas beyond your job title.

3.2 Mitigate Risk

In practical terms, eliminating risk is very expensive and often impossible, so it's important to understand that mitigating risk is not a binary decision, there are levels to it. A simple mitigation can be a document defining what will be done in case a certain feature breaks, while a complex solution might be to implement an automated self-healing capability for the system. Both solutions mitigate the same risk but with very different impact on users and engineers. In between these two, there are an infinite number of other solutions, so the job is not only prioritizing what risk to mitigate but also deciding how much of it should be mitigated. There's no single answer to that, it's all going to depend on the very specific context your business and product are in and even different people will have different opinions on how to proceed. **The key is always balancing cost and benefit, and since risk is the product of likelihood times the impact, you can tackle the problem by either tackling one or both of those variables.** For example, suppose you are building a checkout cart for an ecommerce store, this is a risky feature because you are going to manage everything related to the payment such as security and the credit card transactions. You could manage the risk of something breaking and people not being able to conclude their purchases by building a monitoring system that sends alerts whenever an unusual amount of transactions fail. That way you would be mitigating the risk by reducing the **criticality** of a failure event as you would be able to detect and fix issues faster. But you could also heavily invest in making your infrastructure fail-safe, or perhaps integrate with a more reliable/expensive payment processor, thus reducing the **likelihood** of things breaking.

Mitigating risk is directly dependent on identifying it. It's a common situation that people fail to mitigate risk not because they don't know how to do it, but because they fail to identify it. Known risks are manageable by business decisions and prioritization, unknown risks are just disasters waiting to happen when you least expect. Notice that choosing not to mitigate a certain risk is very different from not knowing what the risks are; in the former, you are in control of the situation while in the latter, you are left to fate. There are two main ways to learn how to identify risks. The first one is by failing over and over until you develop a repertoire of the things that don't work in certain situations. It's a costly but effective method because you are the one suffering the consequences of your own mistakes so your brain easily assimilates how to identify the same situation again in order to avoid it. The second approach is to learn from other people' mistakes. You can do that by reading articles and books, going to conferences, and watching videos, or by learning from seeing coworkers dealing with their mistakes. This is a cheaper method but less effective as it's harder to assimilate and adapt other people's context to yours. Getting involved during incident resolution is a way to learn that combines both approaches by giving you hands-on experience while learning from other people. In all cases, you can only benefit from being capable of identify risk if you employ this skill by actively investing time reviewing your plans and trying to identify what and how things can break. A few minutes of intentional thinking can save a lot of time and money directly wasted on bugs and incidents, and indirectly, on context switching and stress.

There are some techniques that can help you to anticipate what can go wrong. An interesting methodology consists in writing "pre-mortems." While post-mortems (more on post-mortems in the *Learn from mistakes* section) are retrospective documents about problems that already happened, pre-mortems are an analytical exercise of starting from a problem and trying to work backwards into what could lead to it. It's a very effective way for groups and individuals to brainstorm possible failure points of the system they are working on. Another approach is to write playbooks on how to fix problems that are likely to happen. Just like some home appliances have manuals on how to deal with error codes, software teams can write playbooks that list and have instructions on how to fix problems. This kind of playbook has the benefit of empowering more people in the team to act upon a failure or incident, enabling faster responses and therefore making the whole product more resilient. It also makes the operation of the product safer as following instructions is much safer than making up a plan on the go and it reduces risk of human error, especially in a stressful situation. This process of writing a playbook is also beneficial as it's yet another opportunity to reflect on the ways things can fail.

Conversely, a more hands-on way to mitigate risk is by employing fault-tolerance. The idea is to assume every software is prone to breaking in ways that are hard to predict and, with that in mind, design it in a way that reduces impact when problems happen. A good parallel to fault-tolerant software in the physical world are fail-safe devices. For example, elevators are designed in a way that when it loses power, brakes are automatically deployed not letting the cabin fall. There are many ways to make software fault-tolerant; one of the most basic ones is to make extensive use of logs as they can be used to debug problems and in some critical situations even enable recovering lost data. More robust techniques include things like compartmentalizing the software and reducing interdependencies. That way, different features don't interfere with each other and users can keep using a limited version of the product even when some part of the system is broken. It's also possible to have built-in fallback tools and solutions that automatically switch on when a primary solution fails. And features can be designed to self-audit and send alerts when things don't seem right. For data recovery a more appropriate and robust solution than relying on logs is to implement techniques such as Change Data Capture (CDC).

We had a situation in one of Vinta's projects where an application used a secondary database to store metadata about user's actions. These were relevant information but non-critical to the operation of the system. An issue caused by our infrastructure provider during a planned maintenance window took down this secondary database but it didn't affect the main one. Unfortunately, the application code was designed in a way that made the error in the secondary database to affect and break some of the main flows of the product. We evaluated the situation and decided that it was more important to restore the application to users even if that meant losing some of the metadata. So our first step was to comment out all calls to the secondary database and deploy a new version of the application so people could get back to using it. We then deployed a new secondary database, restored the data from a backup and uncommented calls. At this point the

133

application was back to fully operational and the team out of crisis mode so we could take our time to design and build a long-term solution that would prevent the issue from happening again. The final solution was to decouple calls to the secondary database from the main application flow so they would happen asynchronously and not interfere in a downtime situation. This is a good example of how simple techniques can make software more fault-tolerant.

Since many software problems are caused by engineer mistakes, architecture also plays an important role in fault tolerance. All code should be designed to be maintained by engineers that have a lot less context than the person who wrote it initially. If a certain function has a destructive behavior, you should make sure that this is explicit in its name so the person calling it knows straight away that they are dealing with a risky action. Clearly communicate side effects so they don't catch fellow engineers off guard.

Feature toggles (or feature flags) are one of the best techniques to mitigate risk. The idea is to make it easy to switch on and off functionalities in your application on demand. Toggles can be used for many purposes such as launching a new feature, fixing a bug, making a complex migration, or testing a new algorithm. The main goal is to give engineers and product managers more control over when features will go live and also the ability to turn things off in case they are not behaving as expected. In practice, feature toggles are just if/else statements that can be activated or deactivated without the need to deploy a new version of the software. They will usually be controlled by a key-value store database but any tool that allows storing and reading a value will work. For more complex team structures and applications it might be worth contracting a dedicated service to store and manage toggles. In all cases, it's important to keep in mind that the place where toggles are stored needs to be fast as it will be frequently accessed. Another extremely important aspect to keep in mind is that feature toggles can be operated simultaneously and they will often affect each other. It's key that you design the system to work in all combinations of features on and off or you'll risk causing incidents. For that same reason it's important to plan the life cycle of toggles, they should exist to fulfill a goal and should be removed once that goal is met. Feature toggles can introduce a lot of complexity, so in order for the benefits to outweigh the costs and risks, you need to properly manage them.

Integrations with external services are a particularly sensitive part of software and require special attention when it comes to risk mitigation. They are a double-edged sword. They allow you to delegate certain parts of the system to a third party that is going to run and manage things for you, but they also have the downside of you losing some control over them. Which means that when something breaks, your hands are tied and you depend on someone else to fix them. It's not reasonable to assume that things will always work with your integration partners just like it's not reasonable to assume your own system is never going to fail. Take that into consideration when opting to use any external tool that you don't have direct access to the codebase or to the infrastructure and prepare your software to deal with eventual problems from them. What happens with your system when the external integration breaks? Does it go down or your users can still use features but with some limitations? How do you communicate to your users about the problem? Does this impact your contracts with clients? Should you have more than one integration partner so you can automatically switch between them in these situations? There are many techniques to manage this kind of problem; if you want to learn more about them, some of the terms to look for are "circuit breaker" and "kill switches."

Don't take design for granted, even if your team has designers defining the specs of the features you are going to work on, don't abstain from thinking critically about the user experience of what you are developing. Be vocal about the things you think are not clear to the users. One simple example of this is when dealing with features that can lead to destructive actions; sometimes just adding a confirmation modal can save you a lot of trouble.

Pacing your deliveries in small and incremental changes is another great way to mitigate risk. Bugs are inevitable, by avoiding making big changes all at once we are reducing the amount of things that are going to break together and consequently decreasing the impact these will have. We are also making it easier to spot the problem and, in many cases, also making it easier to roll back the changes. The riskier the thing you are doing is, the more you should try to break it into multiple small steps. That approach also has the benefit of improving the code review process by enabling people to focus on smaller scopes at a time and thus increasing the chances of identifying problems. The criticality of the changes you are making should also impact how it's going to be tested before it reaches users. While automated tests are often good enough for most of the code you will be writing, there are situations where they won't be enough to ensure things are going to work in the production environment. Automated unit tests can only take you so far, in critical situations is well worth the effort to invest on a staging environment that has a similar infrastructure and data to the production one.

Keeping this mindset of making small changes is also positive because it allows you to better level your risk mitigation strategy. As we mentioned earlier, risk mitigation is not about completely removing risks but sometimes it's hard to decide how much of it we need to do. By breaking your plans into multiple phases you will be able to see the impact of each change. At some point you might even notice that you already have enough and will be able to avoid spending time and effort on a more complex solution than you needed.

Key takeaways:

- There are levels to mitigating risk, you will need to evaluate your options and balance cost and benefits.

- To mitigate risk you first need to identify it. Actively invest time mapping how things can break.

- Build fault-tolerant features, and write code that makes it harder for your teammates to make mistakes.

- Pay special attention to integrations with external services, your code should expect them to fail from time to time and know how to handle these situations.

- Deploy continuous and incremental changes to the code to facilitate reviewing and reduce risks of catastrophic incidents.

3.3 Trust Nothing

Risk management is a broad topic and there are many different techniques that will help you build a consistent way of ensuring each type of risk, from business to infrastructure, is understood and under control throughout the product life cycle. Each of these techniques will have different levels of complexity and assertiveness, so in certain situations the gains will be well worth the effort, and in other situations it might introduce too much bureaucracy for gains that are not that significant given the business context. For example, hiring a consulting firm to perform a security analysis in your software from time to time is a great way to manage the risk of getting hacked, but depending on the type of software you are working on, it might make very little sense to do it before it has a reasonable user base.

One of the cheapest and easiest ways to manage risk in all phases of product development is by being skeptical. **As an engineer it is essential to build the habit of questioning everything that is not clear to you.** Being skeptical allows you to identify and manage risk regardless of the business context of what you are building. By doing that you will be able to avoid a lot of problems even in projects without mature risk management processes in place. This is a skill that applies to all areas of your work, for example, you shouldn't assume product and design decisions to be error-free. If you have a hunch that something is missing or not looking right, make sure you are going to express that out loud and that you are going to ask questions until someone gives you good answers. Or when you are evaluating architecture and technical decisions of old and new features, you shouldn't settle until everything has a reasonable explanation. Even if the explanation doesn't make sense or if you consider it a bad decision, at least you will have the context needed to evaluate the risks and propose improvements.

Adopting this mindset is especially useful while investigating bugs and reviewing data from dashboards, logs, and reports. Always be critical of the information you are looking at. If what you are seeing doesn't match your expectations, even if it is just by a small fraction, you should look for other sources that can assert the validity of that information. For things that are critical for the business, you should double-check everything even if they are looking right. Use that same skepticism for every new code you deploy to production, that's one of the moments of highest risk in the software development life cycle. Write your code in a way that allows you to verify everything went according to plan. Even when things look right in the interface, review that the flow of the data through the code in the backend was the expected one, check if side effects were properly triggered, check if other parts of the code that have touching points with what you changed did not get affected.

Be careful with biases, things that disprove your expectations are more important than the ones that confirm it. Never assume things are correct until you actively check it. That is especially true when someone makes a question to you. Unless you are sure about the answer don't give people the false sensation of security, confirm you have the right information and then give an assertive answer. Or, if you are not 100% sure about something, make that clear in your answer and, if possible, ask the person to personally double-check the information before they make any important decisions. Notice that this is not about refusing to answer, quite the opposite, speak out the information you have and even your personal beliefs, but don't be afraid to explicitly distinguish what you are certain about and what needs double-checking.

Being skeptical is not about distrusting your teammates, so you should be careful as not to sound confrontational during these conversations. Instead, always frame it as curiosity, a genuine interest to know more about something that you feel you don't fully understand or that you need more context. Say things like "my expectations were that this would behave in X way, why is it doing Y?" and "did you consider Z?" or even "have you tried W?" Instead of telling people that something is wrong try to ask the questions that will lead them to reach the same conclusions you have.

Ponder the criticality of things, things that can lead to significant problems deserve to be scrutinized, but it's ok and often positive to let go of what is not critical. Give visibility about your mental models, explain what information is guiding your train of thought and what assumptions you are making. By doing that you are creating opportunities to learn by identifying the flaws in your understanding of the situation and at the same time assessing and sharing risk with your team.

Key takeaways:

- Question everything that doesn't make sense to you and find out the reasoning behind decisions.

- Don't blindly trust data from a single source, if things are not matching your expectations seek other sources to confirm the information.

- Always review your deliveries after they are live in the production environment.

- Be clear about the level of confidence you have in the answers you give.

- Be careful with how you communicate, your goal should be to generate collaboration, not confrontation.

3.4 Avoid Overengineering

There are multiple ways to write a software that solves a particular problem, some are straight up inefficient, some are mathematically optimal, some work well in certain scenarios but not in others, some are easy to understand, some require a PhD degree, some can be written with minimal number of lines while others require complex architectures. A strategic engineer knows that the ideal solution depends on context, so their job is to understand the domain where the solution is going to operate, learn what the constraints are, and pick a solution that reasonably fits within these parameters. Engineers also understand that constraints change over time so they also consider in their decision the trade-offs of picking a solution according to what they expect to happen, but knowing that it may or may not actually turn out in the predicted way. Many problems in computer science have mathematically proven optimal solutions, conversely in software engineering, it's often impossible to determine what is the best solution for a minimally complex problem. The main reason for that is because frequently it's simply not possible or viable to quantify parameters or precisely measure outputs.

Overengineering is the act of planning, developing, or adopting a solution that is disproportionately more complex or robust than what is needed to be for a given context. Commonly it does not happen out of naivety, it's actually an intentional decision often justified by an urge to be prepared for a situation that is theoretically possible, but that in practice the cost of investment outweighs the probability of it happening or of it significantly impacting the system. In other words, **overengineering comes from employing expensive solutions to prevent problems that are cheap to mitigate in case they materialize**. Notice that a high cost of building or maintaining the solution is the precondition and we are balancing two other parameters to make our decision: cost to mitigate and expected risk [see the decision matrix below]. This misalignment between expectations and reality leads to solutions that are more complex than needed, more time-consuming to implement, and more costly to operate and maintain. As previously said, we should always leverage all the information we have to make our decisions. The problem starts when we prepare for something that is not a business requirement or that we have no factual indication of it happening or generating a significant problem. Other situations that lead to overengineering are: desire to use certain tools or technologies (often newly released ones or that are picking up attention from other engineers), underestimation of the capacity of a tool, overestimation of future demand, miscommunication with stakeholders (that can happen from both ways), and lack of experience with the technology or the business domain.

Overengineering decision matrix

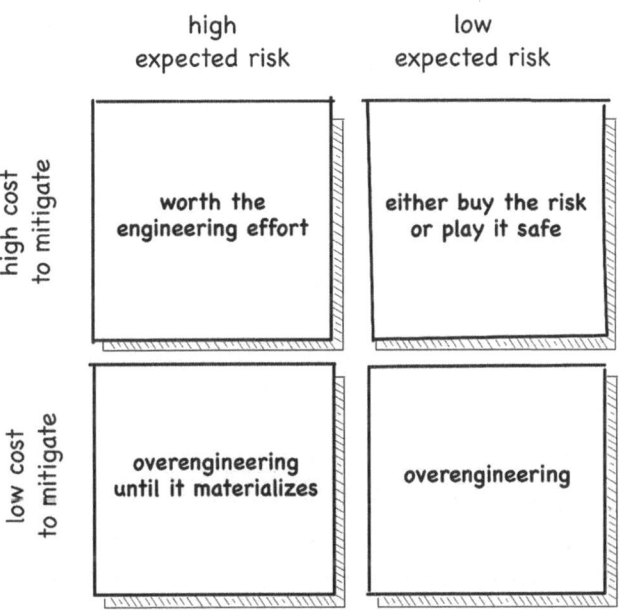

The best vaccine against overengineering is taking decisions based on concrete data and resisting the urge to predict the future. Trying to fix problems that have no indication of actually happening is a bad investment not only because it wastes resources on an unneeded solution but also because you will find out that it's often a game of cat and mouse, the actual bottleneck will show up in some other place that you didn't predict and things will still break. Instead of trying to predict and cover all the possible ways things can break, which is impossible to do, you should focus on making it easy to collect and review data from your system so you have more information to decide what is the best solution and when to employ it. That means that by delaying decisions you are allowing yourself more time to observe and learn from that data and therefore increasing the chances of doing the right investment. The Rule of Three for refactoring is a great example on how delaying decisions is a good idea, by waiting before you've seen a similar problem at least two times and only considering a generalization on the third time you are gathering more information about the problem and ensuring that the more complex, but better solution is actually worth the investment.

Our field of work evolves rapidly and it's only normal that professionals want to be on the cutting edge of available tools; after all, they make our job easier, faster, more efficient, or even just more enjoyable. Unfortunately, this behavior often leads to overengineering. Before adopting a new process, tools, or technology, consider the costs involved, such as the setup and adoption time, the learning curve, and cognitive load and compare it to the short- and long-term benefits. With all things considered, is it still a good investment? Keep in mind that new is not always better and what works for other people might not be the best approach for you or your current context. Most software teams are not dealing with problems at the scale of Google so your team probably needs much simpler solutions than Google needs. Be pragmatic about your decisions and choose wisely what's worth your time and energy and your company's money.

Time and money are the two constraints that are transversal to pretty much all real world projects. Usually all projects, since their very beginning, have a limit on how much money is going to be invested and a rough expectation on when it should be done (whatever the definition of done is). That means that at the very least all engineering decisions are bound by these two constraints. **Engineers don't need a perfect solution, they need one that works and is cost-effective, sometimes these two are the same, most times they are not.** In fact, perfect solutions can harm projects by blowing up budgets or losing time to market. It's usually better to have a quick but imperfect solution released early than to invest too much on a perfect one that still has no guarantee of winning clients. This is again the same pattern we've applied in other contexts throughout this book: first make it work and then make it better, but in this situation only make it better if you actually need to.

Overengineering is a well-known issue in software engineering and many methodologies and popular practices will reference or promote measures to disencourage and counteract it. The widely adopted Lean Startup methodology popularized the concept of Minimum Viable Products (MVPs) as the way to bring business ideas to life. It's baked into the MVP idea that you start by building the smaller product that delivers some value and take it to be tested by real clients as soon as possible, learning from that experience and planning a new cycle of build, measure, and learn from there. Overengineering is clearly an anti-pattern to the Lean Startup approach of building software. Another example is the Agile Manifesto, some of the supporting principles of it include "Our highest priority is to satisfy the customer through early and continuous delivery of valuable software," "Deliver working software frequently, from a couple of weeks to a couple of months, with a preference to the shorter timescale" and "Simplicity, the art of maximizing the amount of work not done, is essential." While not as explicit or directly related, it's also easy to understand how overengineering can go against these ideas. Some well-known expressions within the software engineering community also directly address overengineering, two of the most popular ones are YAGNI (You Aren't Gonna Need It) and KISS (Keep It Simple, Sweetie).

Finally, beware of the cost of software maintenance. It's intuitive to think that the cost of software is only the time it takes to implement it when in reality every added line also introduces a cost of maintenance that is permanent until the project ends or until it's removed. Most people underestimate what software maintenance comprehends. It involves the more obvious cost of fixing bugs and updating things, but it also includes things like the cognitive load of dealing with one more moving part every time you want to change something, managing security, and the learning curve of training people joining the team. More software equals more problems.

Key takeaways:

- Engineering decisions need to leverage many parameters such as technical complexity, team maturity, business context, existing demand, expected demand, risks and costs of mitigation.

- Overengineering is building expensive solutions to prevent easy to mitigate problems with unclear chances of happening.

- Avoid overengineering by postponing high cost decisions until you have reliable data to back it up.

- Start from solutions with the lowest possible cost that meet the requirements, observe how it performs and take your next decisions based on the data you collect.

- Time and money are always going to be important constraints, especially for growing companies and in high competition markets.

3.5 Technical Debt

Technical debt is everything in a software system that is known to be in a less than ideal situation, including infrastructure, code, and product functionality. There are two types of technical debt: intentional and accidental. Intentional debt happens when a piece of code that represents a short-term benefit but that is knowingly problematic for the mid or long term of the product, is consciously introduced to the software. In that situation, technical debt works similarly to money debt, you are going to get something now, which is usually a faster time to ship, but that will need to be paid off with interest in the future, which usually means you are going to need to do some refactoring or a complete rewrite as it starts to become a problem. This is a good type of technical debt because it allows you to make strategic decisions based on business and considering the technical trade-offs. It's also frequently a good opportunity to have meaningful discussions with fellow engineers and product stakeholders about what the priorities are and to get a better understanding of the business goals.

The second type of technical debt actually does not involve the addition of any new code. Accidental debt is generated at the moment someone notices an existing part of the software is incompatible or a drag for current or upcoming goals of the product. Code that was thought to be adequate to the technical and business goals at the time it was written suddenly becomes debt. This can happen due to business factors such as changes to product goals, priorities, or even to the frequency and the way users are interacting with a certain feature. Technical factors are also big generators of accidental technical debt: development tools are constantly evolving and the release of new versions, changes to conventions, or the emergence of new technologies can quickly turn once perfectly good software into technical debt. Even the process of engineers learning new things and growing in their careers can generate debt as they will naturally identify problems with their past decisions. The same happens when someone new joins the team or when there's a handover from one team to another. Whenever you inherit code from other engineers there's always going to be technical debt, both because you don't have all the context about why decisions were made and because each person has their own set of skills that would lead them to do things differently anyway. Avoid using this as a platform to undermine the work of others, it's not strategic and you gain nothing from doing that. You are much more likely to learn something and avoid making mistakes if you adopt a humble attitude and try to understand why and what decisions led the software to that state. Also accept that dealing with "bad code" (often known as "code written by other people") is just part of the job. Focus on making a plan to promote the changes you think that are necessary, and more importantly, in executing that plan which is always the hardest part.

Just like money debt, technical debt compounds and over time you will be forced to pay it whether it's by finally finding time to invest in fixing the problems or by the effects accumulated debt has on the product and the development flow. Not paying debt leads to software that is difficult and slow to change so adding new features and fixing bugs take a lot more time than it should. This leads to ever more frustrated stakeholders as simple things now take unreasonable time to get done. Over time, the product also tends to become unreliable, buggy, and risky to operate. Bad solutions are added on top of each other in order to overcome problems without the need to invest time in designing and implementing proper solutions. Code gets coupled and now to fix one debt you need to change five other things that depend on it. Every time you postpone the problem it becomes even harder and costlier to solve. By now it should be clear that **it's impossible and also not strategic for a project to have zero technical debt but simply ignoring it is also not an economically smart decision for any team with long term goals.** The best we can do as engineers is to learn how to manage technical debt as part of the usual development process, making conscious decisions based on context and known trade-offs, and periodically reassess these decisions.

A project I was working on for one of Vinta's clients had a deadline to launch a new feature. But, for it to work properly we needed to make performance improvements to another existing part of the system. Because of the short timespan there was not enough time to write the code for the feature and also make the improvements. To remediate the situation, we proposed to increase our infrastructure costs by bumping the memory and CPU specs of the machines we were using to make up for the inefficiencies of the code so we could launch the feature and work on performance improvements later on. By doing that we were quite literally buying a technical debt that allowed us to meet the deadline and also buying the team time to pay the debt with the benefit of relieving the pressure and stress of doing things in a rush.

Fixing technical debt is rarely something easy to do, but the main reason for that is not usually technical. In real world projects, there are many forces pushing you to postpone things just a little more. Over time, problems keep accumulating until something breaks catastrophically and suddenly everyone is questioning how things got to that point. **As engineers, the most important thing is understanding that we own technical debt, there's no one in the project other than us that can properly evaluate the risks of the code we wrote.** It's not the role of business and product stakeholders to ask if we want to pause everything and spend a whole quarter just refactoring and fixing technical debt, their job is to keep pushing us into delivering value to the users. Unless we explicitly explain what, why, and when we need to work on technical debt, they will rightfully just keep expecting us to deliver more features as fast as we can. It's our responsibility to inform stakeholders about what we need to do in order to keep things running smoothly and the risks and consequences of not doing it. But we need to do it in a way that resonates with their goal of delivering value to the user. For instance, when you say that you need some time to improve the deployment process of the project, it communicates very little about the value you are adding. But if you rephrase that to something like "The current process is slow and requires too much manual intervention which has lead to X incidents in the past month. It's important to automate it to make it faster and more reliable especially as the team grows," it gives stakeholders a lot more information about how that work is going to impact the product and a better understanding of the risks of not doing it. That way, it becomes easier to compare and prioritize that demand with everything else in the backlog. Doing a good job making a case for the needed work on technical debt doesn't mean it's going to be smooth sailing from there on, expect pushbacks and be prepared to negotiate. Defending the codebase is an ongoing effort, there will always be things to improve and you need to work with (not against) other stakeholders in order to find the right balance between keeping the lights on and adding new features.

So how do we tackle technical debt? There's a great article by Matt Greenberg and Keya Patel titled "Tech Debt Isn't a Burden, It's a Strategic Lever for Success" that answers this question with all the depth it needs considering many of the nuances it requires. I'll try to summarize some of the main concepts here so you can grasp the idea. The first thing to consider is the size of the debt, acute debt is low effort and can be fixed quickly, this type of debt is a lot easier to deal with, you just get it done as you move forward with your work. Systemic debt is much bigger and requires a lot of effort to get fixed so it requires prioritization, planning, and dedicated time. So beyond the technical challenge of fixing the debt there's the challenge of finding the right time to do it in between the busy schedule of any product team. The five variables you are going to balance in order to prioritize it are

- Confidence: How likely is it this debt going is to lead to bigger problems?

- Time: How long will it take for it to become an unmanageable issue?

- Impact to user: How much or how likely is this going to impact end users?

- Sequence: Does it block the team from achieving some goal?

- Accumulated debt: How much debt have you accumulated?

The answer to these questions along with the business stage of your project should give you a good framework to think strategically and decide with other project stakeholders how you are going to manage technical debt throughout the project life cycle.

Another interesting way to tackle technical debt is to pick your own personal battles to fight. Although this is usually a good way for you to fix issues that are annoying you and that might also be bothering teammates, it requires a lot of discipline and responsibility as it shouldn't impact roadmap tasks. If you are going to spare some time to work on these projects, make sure it's either very small or that you are going to break it down into small deliverables so you can gradually build your way into your goal with no major impact to other activities. But other than that it's a lot of fun to have this kind of personal goals and results will usually be appreciated by your teammates.

Key takeaways:

- Leverage intentional debt to gain short term benefits but don't forget that it will need to be paid later on.

- Accidental debt is inevitable, avoid criticizing others and focus your energy on fixing them.

- Communicate the impact of debt to the product to and to the development flow and practice negotiating with stakeholders.

- Fix the issues that bother you, but be careful managing time investment so it doesn't affect your roadmap deliveries.

3.6 Consider the Non-functional Requirements

Non-functional requirements (NFRs) are the parts of the software that, although necessary for the operation of the system, are not directly related to the business logic of it. For instance, a functional requirement to a video streaming service is that it plays the video in the users' browser, but what if the service takes too long to load or easily goes down under any small spike in demand, is it really fulfilling its role? The goal of the software is to provide value to its users, it doesn't matter if certain features exist if, in practice, it doesn't work when users need them. Functional requirements describe what the feature does in a "naive way," it answers the question "is the system capable of executing the task?" Non-functional requirements answer a different question "will users be able to use the feature whenever they need it?" It's a subtle difference but an important one because it determines if, in the end, users will accomplish what they need.

Considering and planning for the non-functional requirements of what you build must always be part of your risk analysis. Each system has its own constraints so you need to understand the business and who are its users in order to plan what needs more attention, what can be addressed in a later moment and what is not relevant to that particular context. Here's a list of some common non-functional requirements in software systems:

- Accessibility: What are the obstacles users might encounter due to personal limitations when using the software? How do you make things easier so that everyone can benefit from the product?

- Availability: Is the system up and running when users need it?

- Cost-effectiveness: Is the infrastructure you are planning to use in accordance with the company's financial expectations? How does it affect the final pricing to users? Are you dimensioning resources (such as memory, CPU, database size) effective according to the expectations of the software usage?

- Fault tolerance: When something breaks, does it take down the whole system? Could failure be handled in a smoother way or in a way that has less impact on the user?

- Security: Does the system attend basic industry security practices? Are there any security practices that are specific to the domain you are working on? Is the development team trained on security practices? Which are the critical vulnerabilities that can affect the system?

- Recoverability: How hard is it to restore the system when it breaks?

- Scalability: Can the system adapt to surges in demand? Is it designed to adapt to business growth?

- Extensibility: Does the code architecture enable for new features to be added with low effort and risk of breaking the existing ones?

- Developer Experience (DX): Is the development setup easy for team members to do their best work? Is it easy for new members of the team to onboard?

These are just some examples of the things that are intrinsic to the development of any software, there are of course an infinite number of other aspects that may or may not be relevant to a given business context.

Notice how concerns related to the maintenance of the software from the engineer's perspective are also considered non-functional requirements. Now that we have a better understanding of what non-functional requirements are and their importance, let's dig a little deeper into two topics that are common to most software products operating in a real world environment: observability and performance.

Side note: the term "non-functional requirements" is not very descriptive of what it means and because of that some people have been pushing for it to be rebranded as "cross-functional requirements" (CFRs). This new term, while not fully adopted yet, provides a better sense on how it addresses expectations from a diverse set of technical and non-technical perspectives.

Key takeaways:

- Think beyond the feature specs; what are the technical and non-technical aspects that will make the feature to successfully deliver value to all users in all desired conditions?

- You don't need to address everything but it's important that you consciously choose what should be covered now and what you are leaving for later when demand catches up.

3.7 Observability

Observability is the practice of tooling a system in order to gain visibility over its components and behavior. The goal is to ensure things are executing according to expectation with regard to factors such as availability, performance, rate of failure, and security to facilitate debugging and, in extreme cases, to recover state that was lost due to an incident. It can be used to track user experience, goals defined by the business and even to uphold contractual requirements. Observability is one of the most important assets for engineers to manage risk, and it does it from many perspectives; it enables investigating and fixing ongoing problems, identifying issues before they happen through alerting, and planning future growth in order to dimension infrastructure accordingly. There are many approaches to observability such as logging, tracing, monitoring, and alerting. The best approach will vary depending on what you want to achieve but most applications require a combination of tools and techniques to accomplish their observability goals.

Logging is the most basic and common approach to observability, its goal is to record the history of your application. The most frequent mistake people make is to only think about it when problems arise and the only thing they can do is to regret not having more visibility over some part of the system that would be key to solving the problem. In order to be useful, it needs to be an integral part of building features, just throwing text messages around your code is not the best way to do it as it often leads to the cluttering of worthless information. It requires looking into the future so it requires planning, just like you plan application flows and performance requirements. Logging requires an exploratory process to identify what information is really going to be useful later on when you are investigating a bug or an incident. How can the application break? What data will allow me to identify what was impacted and how it was impacted? What do I need to reconstruct the system state at a certain point in time? These are some of the questions that you need to ask while planning and the answers will help you find the right information to log.

Logs are only useful if you can easily analyze them when they are needed; that means all logs from an application and its related systems should be centralized in a single place and that it should be easy to filter for time period, terms, and source. Logs that are not easy to consume or that are scattered over multiple locations are a nightmare to deal with, especially in a crisis situation where you are under pressure and have a lot of things to manage.

Another important consideration about logs is security. It's a major concern for your application and your users in case someone gets hold of your logs, so be careful about how they are stored and who has access to them. At the same time, no team is exempt from a security breach so it's important to be careful with what goes into logs. Never log Personally Identifiable Information (PII), these are any piece of information that can identify who are the users of your system, things such as names, email, phone numbers and addresses, instead use internal ids to point to individual users. Also make sure that secrets such as passwords, API, and session keys are never exposed in logs, this is a common occurrence when someone forgets to remove a debug statement that accidentally goes to production. If this happens, immediately rotate the leaked keys and invalidate the old ones. Depending on where in the world your users are and the kind of data you are dealing with, some regulations may apply, so do some research to make sure you are following the right set of practices.

Logs are good for investigating single events and troubleshooting; however, they may not be the best option for displaying general status of the system or showing aggregated state. For this, metrics are much more effective. This type of monitoring consists of aggregating data from various parts of the application and its infrastructure and displaying this information in a way that is easy to visualize and to spot anomalies. This practice is frequently referred to as Application Performance Monitoring (APM) and there are many tools that specialize in it. These tools usually require little effort to integrate with your application and can provide aggregated views of the data as well as single out events for you to analyze step by step what happened during the execution of the code. The metrics you should monitor will vary depending on the type of application you are developing. Common infrastructure metrics include: CPU and memory usage in servers, network traffic, disk IO, database query response time, and latency. Web applications usually need to monitor things like: endpoint response time, throughput of requests, duration of batch jobs and error rate. Other types of applications might need to observe power consumption, graphics performance, data collection and CPU temperature for example.

Especially for distributed applications, it's important that you can observe as data moves across systems; that ability is called tracing. Tracing consists in generating a token that will be passed throughout the different parts of your application being tagged to logs and that can be used to reconstruct the sequence in which operations happened. That in combination with centralized logging will make it much easier and save you a great deal of time when debugging. Without these two techniques, it's safe to say that it would be impossible to do it in any reasonably big application.

So far, we've talked about metrics that are measured from within the application, they require special access to the infrastructure and code in order to gather detailed information on how each component is behaving, but there's another approach to monitoring which gathers data from the perspective of an actual user; it's called synthetic monitoring. It consists of defining a sequence of operations that are automatically run and simulate a user performing a task in the system. The advantage of this approach is that it's much more accurate in reporting the true experience of your end users using the system, confirming that they can actually complete an activity in the expected time.

For some applications external integrations are critical, if this is the case for you, it's often a good idea to monitor these dependencies and write software that is resilient to failure or at least define a plan of what to do in case these integrations stop working. It's also a good idea to build dashboards with the most important metrics from their system so it's possible to have an overview of how things are with a quick glance.

The techniques presented so far can be categorized as Active Observability. While it's extremely important to build visibility through metrics, if you stop there, the product will always depend on users to report a problem before someone can use logs and metrics to find the root cause and fix the issue. Or even depend on a specific tech team watching dashboards all the time.

To improve on this we need passive observability. Alerts exist to bridge that gap and enable a system that self-reports when something is not behaving as expected. Most of the metric tools available in the market also provide a mechanism to trigger alerts once a certain data point reaches or goes over a certain threshold. That signal can be connected to an action such as sending an email, a message to the team chat tool, calling a phone, or even making a request to an endpoint in another system. It might seem trivial to set up alerts but it actually requires some considerations in order to make it effective. Make sure you pay attention to the thresholds of your alerts, having a low threshold allows you to be notified before things actually break which may allow you to fix the issue before it becomes noticeable to the users. But it might as well lead to a situation where you are constantly dismissing alerts because they are not yet critical. It's fundamental that you always treat alerts as critical events. If you start ignoring them and don't take immediate action, they become useless and become a source of noise. Ignored alerts are not only unhelpful, but they can also hide other alerts that might be truly important. That's also why it's necessary to have a routine of tuning your alerts, making them more akin to how the system evolves over time. When you don't treat alerts with the consideration they need, the result is a team that stops paying attention which leads to incidents that could've been prevented.

Different metrics should have different policies, and not all metrics need to trigger an alert; you will need to plan a strategy that makes sense for your application and business context. But in most cases, you should be tracking basic infrastructure metrics such as CPU, memory, and latency between components as these are clear indicators of slowdowns and outages. Lastly, consider how alerts are going to be sent. Email messages are rarely effective to communicate critical events as it's not reasonable (and counterproductive) to expect engineers to be constantly checking their inboxes, but they might work for less critical issues that can wait a few hours to be fixed. Using the team chat tool is slightly better than email for critical situations, especially if people have it installed in their phones but it is still not ideal as it's easy to ignore or dismiss notifications. The best approach is usually to use an on-call rotation tool, it allows setting up a phone call rotation schedule where it tries to contact one person after another until someone acknowledges the incident. This is especially useful outside business hours because you don't want the whole team being notified every time an alert goes off, someone can kick off an initial investigation and escalate the problem to other team members as needed.

Observability is an extensive subject and one that is frequently overlooked, people often only care about it when it's too late and they need information that cannot be recovered anymore. It's a key feature of any well-built software and it's a special one because it needs to be transversal to everything else you build otherwise it easily loses its purpose. In many ways, it is a concept that is trivial to understand which may steer some people to think it's easy to build their own monitoring system, but doing it reliably, especially at scale, is very hard. At the same time it's a solved problem, there's no point in reinventing the wheel, try the many solutions available and choose the one that best suits your technical and business needs.

Key takeaways:

- Plan your logs just like you plan your features. Consider what can go wrong and how logs can help you investigate and fix problems.

- Centralize logs from all sources in a single place, be careful with PII and use traces to easily observe information flowing through different parts of the system.

- Use metrics to visualize the global state of the system, identifying unusual behavior and estimating future demand.

- Alerts should only be triggered in critical situations and should prompt immediate actions from the team.

- Build an escalation policy so you don't have your whole team being notified all at once.

3.8 Performance

Whether you think about it or not, performance is an intrinsic part of all software you write; for any real world application there's always going to be an upper limit on how much load it can take. If you are not actively thinking about performance it either means that you are dealing with a low demand software or that it's very likely that things will break and you will be caught off guard. Nonetheless, thinking about performance does not mean building software that can withstand any load, it means attending the current and the planned demand. An important part of engineering is being cost-effective, and preparing for any possible demand would cost a lot on hardware provisioning and in engineer's time to plan, develop, and maintain such a solution. It makes no sense to expect a product with a couple hundred users to be built in a way that, with no change or intervention, can handle hundreds of thousands of users, unless there's a clear expectation that this kind of growth will happen in the near future.

The key to a healthy, performant system relies on two principles: monitoring and performance testing. As we discussed before, observability is basic to systems of all sizes and should be your starting point when thinking about performance. Whether you are writing a new feature or fixing an existing one that is abnormally slow, it's easy to start guessing what is the source of the problem based on superficial code analysis or gut feeling. Don't fall for that, when you are working in the dark it's easy to end up wasting time on things that look important but have little impact, or that are a lot less significant when compared to other existing issues. The guiding principle to balancing your investment on performance is working based on data and fighting the urge to rely on instinct. Application Performance Monitoring (APM) software is widely available and is in most cases trivial to set up and start collecting data. It will give valuable insight on the most time-consuming parts of your application and within those what are the operations that most contribute to the problem. With a few clicks you should be able to identify whether your problem is related to an inefficient database query, a slow API request, or if your application is demanding too much CPU usage.

Monitoring allows prioritizing the work so less effort leads to a bigger impact. The Pareto principle is one of the most important things you should be using as an engineer, it states that "80% of consequences come from 20% of the causes." Suppose a certain service in your application is spending 9 seconds querying the database and 1 second processing the data. Suppose you want to make this service run faster, you can either focus your efforts in making fewer or faster database queries or in improving your data processing algorithms. If you decide to invest your time writing the perfect algorithm, the best you can do is to make the overall performance of the service 1 second faster, only a 10% improvement. But if you invest your time tuning the database queries, it's likely that simpler improvements will result in a bigger overall performance impact. A great way to observe how the Pareto principle works in practice is by plotting the frequency of usage of services or features of your system in a histogram, ordering by the most used to the least used. It's typical that you will end up with a *long tail distribution* signaling that a few items are responsible for the vast majority of the interaction in the system. The same goes, for example, if you plot the average time web endpoints take to respond or background jobs take to run. An interesting metric for performance analysis arises from multiplying the frequency and the duration of data points as it can be used as an indicator of the impact different parts of the application have on the system and it can be very useful in helping to prioritize performance investment.

Long tail distribution

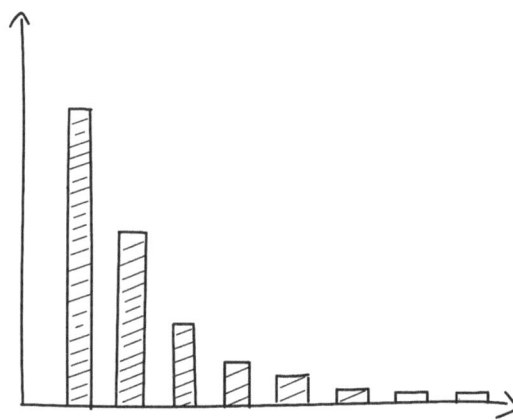

Since we are talking about graphs as a way to visualize performance, it's important to be attentive about what is the information you are plotting in order to not be misled into the wrong conclusions. We are trained through life to think that averages are a great way to aggregate data and it is in fact very useful in many situations. But averages hide important information that should be considered in a performance analysis. Let's take, for example, the distribution of the response time for a particular web endpoint, in other words, let's take the response time of all the requests to this endpoint and plot it in a histogram that has frequency in the y axis and the time it took to execute on the x axis. This graph can take many shapes, a common one is known as the *normal distribution* or "bell shape." In this situation, taking the average of response times of this endpoint would give you a value that is equal or very similar to the most frequent value of the distribution. Since most values are condensed within a small range of the graph, the average is a good representation of the data.

Normal distribution

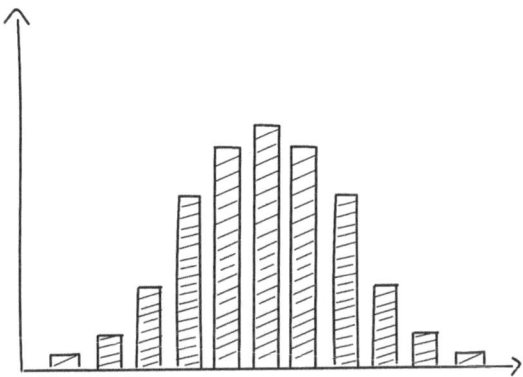

But suppose you have a situation where 90% of the time the endpoint responds faster than 1 second but 10% of the time it takes more than 1 minute. Now the average of all data points would not by itself give you much information about how this endpoint is behaving and wouldn't be very helpful in your investigation to why some users are complaining the system is slow even though it looks fine for most people.

Multimodal distribution

A great tool to improve this kind of analysis is using percentiles, not just averages when it comes to performance. Instead of just saying that X endpoint has an average response time of 600ms, you can also add the information that its 90 percentile (or 90p) is 200ms, meaning that 90% of the time it responds faster or equal to 200ms. Graphs with percentiles provide much more information than just averages and it's a good idea to track at least the 50p and the 90p, but you can tweak these values to the context of your application. Percentiles are also great for communication as it makes it easy to convey to teammates in simple terms how a distribution looks like. In the previous example, it's easy to deduce, for instance, that the topmost 10% of the requests take a lot longer to respond because they are significantly contributing to the average time, an information that can be extremely valuable when investigating the root cause of the problem.

While monitoring allows fixing the performance of the code that is already live for users, performance testing allows benchmarking scenarios in a controlled environment. It consists in using automated software (a probing tool) to generate a load that can be shaped to replicate how the system is expected to be used or even to force it beyond its limits. The advantage is that it can provide visibility to how your system behaves under certain types of load, how much load it can take and what breaks first (the bottlenecks) in these high demand situations. It allows you to fix things before your users are impacted by slowdowns or downtimes. From that perspective performance testing might look like a better solution than monitoring, but the problem is that no matter what technique you use, it's impossible to simulate every way users (or attackers) will behave so it's not a replacement for monitoring, it's a complement. When running tests, you will need to define what is the load and the parameters the probing tool will use. This includes things like what parts of the system will be probed, if there's a particular set of steps it should follow, what is the content and size of the payload and how many requests will be made during the session. Some of the common reasons to run performance tests include evaluating what is the maximum load an application can take while responding within a desired threshold, submitting it to stress and see what breaks and benchmarking a new or changed feature comparing results to confirm things improved or at least didn't get worse. You will need to adapt your benchmarking environment and probing tool setup depending on what you want to achieve.

The environment you are using to run your performance tests should reproduce the production environment as closely as possible, otherwise there's a high chance your results will look very different from how your real application behaves. There are two parts to this: the first is reproducing the infrastructure, that includes using a hardware of similar or as close as possible capacity as your production setup and deciding how to deal with external integrations. Ideally it should make calls to external integrations just like the real application because you will have a more accurate result, but this is often too risky or simply not possible. In that case, try at least to mock or simulate the behavior of the external service. For instance, if you are going to mock an integration that is expected to be slow, you can make your application sleep for some time to replicate what is expected to happen in production. The other part is populating the application with data that is similar to the data in the production setup. One way to do this is simply by cloning your production database, but that is usually not a good idea as it can increase the risk of leaking customer data, violate privacy laws and produce incidents such as sending incorrect emails or making accidental requests to integrations. Another way is to generate your own fake data to populate the database; in that case the data should look as similar as possible to the real production data but doing this is not trivial. There are open source libraries that can help you with the task of generating names, dates, numbers, and addresses, but making it in a way that is consistent with your application business rules requires some effort. The other approach is to start from your production database and anonymize all the Personally Identifiable Information (PII) so there's no risk of having real users data in the test environment. All approaches have pros and cons, evaluate what makes sense to your technical limitations and business constraints and pick the one that works best for you.

There are three key concepts that are tightly related to performance and worth knowing about because of how common they are: N+1, Big-O, and caching. N+1 is an issue related to database data retrieval and it commonly happens in applications using an Object Relational Mapper (ORM) tool where there's an abstraction layer for developers to fetch data without explicitly writing SQL queries. In this situation, the developer is fetching data for an object that is linked to multiple other instances resulting in multiple queries to the database that linearly increase with the number of items and generating a performance issue as the application grows. The name N+1 comes from this behavior of doing one query for the root object and N others for each of the related instances. The solution to this problem is to fetch all related objencts (N) in a single query before starting to process the data.

Big-O is a notation to convey the magnitude of the computational time required to run an algorithm. A program that always takes a fixed amount of time to run regardless of how many items it's processing is deemed as $O(1)$, meaning it runs in a constant time. If the time to run the program grows linearly with the number of items it's processing, we classify it as an $O(n)$ problem. Counting the number of items with value greater than 10 in an array or varying size is an example of a $O(n)$ algorithm. But if your want to generate a table with the product of all numbers in that array, that algorithm will need to do n*n operations so it will be classified as $O(n^2)$. The key concept is that for large numbers of items it makes a huge difference if your program runs on $O(n^2)$ or $O(n)$, and learning how to evaluate your code is great to help you improve performance and to communicate with your peers.

Lastly, caching is a technique to store data that is either slow to query or slow to process, in a place where it can be quickly accessed, usually a "key-value" database or directly in the computer memory. There are many situations where caching can speed up applications by orders of magnitude, making otherwise complex to run in O(1). The problem with it is that when you have two [or more] copies of the same data in your system you create a situation where any changes need to be applied to all the copies of the data in order to keep them updated. This leads to the common and well-documented problem of "cache-invalidation", or in other words, how to determine when a cached value is no longer valid and needs to be fetched again or re-calculated. All of these three concepts are not simple and my goal here was just to provide you with an initial introduction to them. If you are not acquainted with them It's well worth the investment to study more about them.

When planning for performance, remember to include some slack both when defining thresholds for alerts and when evaluating performance test results. Make sure your alerts notify your team before things start to break, while there's still time to fix them. It's good to know that database memory usage is at 100% but if you were receiving alerts that it was frequently reaching 70% you could have migrated to a more capable infrastructure earlier and avoided an outage. If you expect to have one thousand simultaneous users due to a planned event, perhaps you should test if the application can take two thousand users. The goal is to reduce the risk of incidents and also to avoid falling into the vicious cycle of only investing in performance when things are in a critical state.

There's no absolute reference value for performance, it's actually tightly linked to the user experience, what is good will depend on technical, business, and user expectation constraints. It's also interesting to notice that performance and user experience are concepts that feed into each other; performance enables different user experiences and a particular user experience triggers different performance expectations. For example, in a data export feature, users probably expect that after clicking an export button the download starts instantaneously, but if exports are sent via email perhaps they wouldn't care as much if it took a couple of minutes. By tweaking how things are shown and what data is displayed in the interface you can make the job of optimizing performance a lot harder or a lot easier. So keep that in mind; perhaps sometines the best approach is not to focus energy optimizing your database or building a complex caching solution, sometimes you can just hide some information or load it in a separate request with little or no impact on user experience. Lastly, your software does not need to scale indefinitely, instead of wasting time making all features perfectly performant, focus on collecting data, aligning expectations with stakeholders and being clear about what the limitations are. Everything is a trade-off, and your job is to manage risk according to technical and business constraints.

Key takeaways:

- All systems have a capacity limitation, performance implies hardware and engineering costs so it needs to be planned according to reasonable demand expectations.

- It's easy to make wrong guesses about bottlenecks, use metrics to ensure you are tackling the actual source of the issue.

- Leverage the law of Pareto to focus your efforts on the things that have the most potential to generate impact.

- A lot of relevant information can be hidden on averages, use percentiles for better visualizing the shape of the data.

- Use probing tools to test how your application behaves under different types of load.

- Study the Big-O notation, make use of caching [but be careful with its traps], and avoid the N+1 problem.

- Ensure your system operates with a safe margin so you can identify and fix performance issues before they generate incidents.

- Consider how the UX impacts performance and leverage UX to improve the perception of performance.

3.9 Learn from Mistakes

Knowing that managing risk doesn't mean not taking risks, it's easy to infer that it is natural and expected that all software will have problems and no team is exempt from dealing with incidents from time to time. Although these problems are expected to happen, it's not strategic to keep failing over and over due to the same known issue, so it would be a waste of opportunity if failures didn't lead to learning and improvement. It's easy for individuals to learn from their own mistakes; the challenge for a team is how to turn that individual learning into collective growth so the team as a whole and the product become more robust and don't fall into the same issues again.

Sharing knowledge is easier said than done, especially during a crisis situation, everyone's natural way of dealing with incidents is to focus on getting things fixed as soon as possible so they can get back to whatever they were doing before. It takes a conscious effort to recognize the importance and organize what you learned so others can also benefit from it. Building a culture where these learnings are constantly feeding back to the team is the first step. This can be done in multiple ways and teams should mix and match approaches until they find what works best for them. It can be as simple as using retrospective meetings to talk about these learnings, or having an exclusive ceremony where engineers can share and discuss in more depth technical challenges. Writing collaborative documents where people can open discussion threads and add comments and suggestions is also great and it has the advantage of being async and generating a historical register that can always be referenced back to. At the same time, if your team doesn't have a good async work culture, it's easy for this kind of document to become just a bureaucracy that doesn't achieve the goal of collective growth. In that case, it doesn't mean it's not a good idea to use written documents but perhaps that they should also be brought for discussion during synchronous moments. Regardless of how you do it, it's essential that the team is in accordance to the prime directive of retrospectives "regardless of what we discover, we understand and truly believe that everyone did the best job they could, given what they knew at the time, their skills and abilities, the resources available, and the situation at hand."

A step beyond that is using a standardized post-mortem process where it becomes a formal practice of the team to always write documents in a pre-defined format after all incidents. Post-mortems are usually divided into sections and commonly include information like the severity of the incident, a timeline of all the events from the moment the incident was identified to the moment it was resolved, a list of the things that were positive during the process of resolving the problem and a list of the things that didn't work as well, a root cause analysis of the problem, and a list of next steps with the short- and long-term actions the team needs to take in order to avoid new occurrences of the problem. These documents should be dated and stored in a common place where it's easy for everyone in the team to access. They can also be used as a way to build trust through transparency, especially when incidents affect corporate customers. Some companies publish a version of their most relevant post-mortems openly in their blog or send them via email to users.

As important as sharing knowledge amongst the team is to enhance the product so it itself becomes more robust. That can be done by improving the architecture of the codebase so it's harder for engineers to make the same mistakes, even if they don't have the full context of past incidents. Just building a knowledge base and expecting people to remember things by heart is a naive strategy. Over time the amount of documents will keep growing to a size that is not reasonable for engineers to keep up with everything. In addition, software is constantly evolving so documents naturally become outdated. If this is hard for the people that are already in the team, remember that we need to account for new people joining in. It's unreasonable to expect that newcomers will be able to quickly absorb all that information. A more effective way to prevent bugs and incidents from happening is to build guardrails into the software. These guardrails can be built in many different forms, a simple example is naming a function in a way that clearly alerts about the risks of using it (e.g., "DANGEROUS_update_user_profile"). Rust and Go are examples of languages that employ this technique. Other ideas include requiring an explicit confirmation before executing some code and hiding complex operations behind a more friendly interface that simplifies things for the most common use cases. The idea is that you make it harder for other engineers to make mistakes.

Lastly, it's important to evaluate what can improve on the team's risk management skills. If the problem happened due to a known risk, the team should review if there was a problem with the risk assessment. Sometimes there's nothing that could be done differently, the team opted to prioritize other things that were more important at the moment leaving it to chance for known issues to happen. But when things fail due to unknown risks, the team should review their individual and collective practices in order to identify where the failure points are and to empower and train people to be more critical and careful going forward.

Key takeaways:

- Every failure is an opportunity to learn.

- Build a culture of sharing knowledge so the whole team learns from each other's mistakes.

- Use post-mortems as a tool to discuss what happened, identify root causes, and discuss short- and long-term improvements.

- Build guardrails into the code that prevent engineers from making common mistakes.

- Develop your own risk assessment skills and train teammates so they too can identify and prevent pitfalls.

3.10 References and Further Reading

- "Tech Debt Isn't a Burden, It's a Strategic Lever for Success" by Matt Greenberg and Keya Patel `https://www.reforge.com/blog/managing-tech-debt`

- "Technical Debt Quadrant" by Martin Fowler `https://martinfowler.com/bliki/TechnicalDebtQuadrant.html`

- "Web Application Monitoring Best Practices" by Andriy Obrizan `https://leanylabs.com/blog/web-monitoring-best-practices/`

- "RICE Scoring Model" `https://www.productplan.com/glossary/rice-scoring-model/`

CHAPTER 4

Strategic Teamwork

In a connected world with competitive and fast-changing markets, it's rare for a solo engineer to build a product that stays relevant in the long term. In most situations you are going to need a team in order to consistently build something to a large audience, especially if your are building

© Filipe Ximenes 2024
F. Ximenes, *Strategic Software Engineering*, https://doi.org/10.1007/979-8-8688-0995-8_4

enterprise software. Doing effective work and growing a career in software requires developing the skills necessary to work a group. You can be the best programmer and master the discipline to deliver high-quality and high-performing software, but if you are not able to collaborate with other people in your organization, it's likely that your work won't have as much impact or deliver the expected value to users.

Strategic engineers understand that their success is directly linked to the success of their team and that a successful product is the main performance indicator of a team. In a company these metrics of success are deeply related, caring about the product and the team is as important as caring about your individual career. Because of that, improving how you interact and collaborate with teammates is as important as mastering programming languages and learning algorithms.

4.1 The Success of the Team Is the Success of the Product

The goal of any software is to deliver value to users or to an organization. The term "value" in this statement is intentionally vague because it can mean different things to different customers, businesses. The definition of value can also change over time due to changes in people's expectations and market conditions. Even what is considered success will frequently mean different things depending on context. The most obvious form of success for a business is generating revenue. But as we discussed in the *Own your career* section, revenue is not always the short-term goal for a company. Understanding what success means is the first thing a software team needs to do before they can start writing any code. To do that, they will need to gather knowledge about the business domain they are working on, but it's equally important to understand why they are building it, what are the short-, mid-, and long-term goals and expectations the project's leadership has for it.

It's always better, when possible, to benchmark team progress and the success of work using metrics. In a for-profit company, the amount of money a product or feature generates is always going to be the ultimate way to measure the value delivered in the long term, but as software engineers, most of the time we will rarely have direct access to that kind of information. To compensate for that, it's often possible to find some other proxy metric such as the engagement of users in a certain part of the product or to collect qualitative feedback data, for example. In larger companies where each team specializes in a smaller part of the product, it's going to be harder or even impossible to directly link results to the work of a specific team; in that situation, it's useful to come up with metrics that your team can directly impact and that can be linked to mid-term business goals. To do that you should involve business stakeholders that can contribute and validate your plans. Beyond just identifying the parameters of success, this process of debating with business stakeholders has other benefits. It will frequently generate alignment, calibrate expectations, and put everyone in the team in the same page and mood to do their best work.

Your team can only be as successful as the product you are building. Although as engineers we have many ways to measure our work with things such as performance metrics, uptime indicators, and the velocity the team ships new features, business leadership will rarely judge success using only these parameters. Business leaders care about business metrics, the things that increase customer satisfaction and directly or indirectly bring in revenue. If the business indicators that are impacted by the work of your team are looking good, it's very likely that the team will be positively evaluated. So does this mean we should ignore any metrics that are not business-related? Of course not, velocity metrics and technical metrics are extremely important because they indicate that the team can deliver in a consistent and reliable way, and that's a precondition to doing anything else. But an equally important part to the equation of a successful team is ensuring that everyone is working on the right thing, and that is whatever has potential to turn the needles of the business metrics in the direction the business people want. **Technical and business metrics go hand in hand, there's no point in having an extremely performant team if they are delivering the wrong product.**

Conversely, it's important to be attentive because there will be times when companies will start caring more about these technical and velocity metrics. That often happens when things are going bad with the business. When business metrics are not matching stakeholders', such as CEOs and investors' expectations, that's often when leadership will start looking around what needs to change, or even worse, what they can cut to reduce costs. Teams should always keep track of their own performance and proactively find ways to reduce inefficiencies, remove bottlenecks, and increase delivery throughput. Frameworks such as DORA and SPACE can give pointers to what parts of the development cycle your team can measure in order to identify inefficiencies and improve performance. They were developed based on large scale empirical studies with software teams and are what we have closer to scientific knowledge on this topic. We will not dive into them as this is a complex topic that requires dedicated focus beyond the scope of this book, but I encourage you to go research more about them. In any case, more important than picking a certain framework it's to align expectations with managers and other stakeholders, as they might have a different perspective on what performance is and how it should be measured. There isn't yet an industry consensus on what is the best or right way to measure the performance of software teams. The best you can do is to get acquainted with what are the tools available and promote the discussion with your team.

The goal of software teams is to deliver products, not code. Code is an unfortunate requirement of software products: it's hard to build, hard to maintain, and it requires specialized and expensive personnel to do the work. From the users' point of view, and consequently the business point of view, if there was some other cheaper and reliable way to solve their problems they would never choose to have a single line of code in their products. Of course this statement is not literal, it is just an extrapolation, but the point here is that, as software engineers, we should never think that our primary goal is to write code or even that it is to build features. Our job is to provide value to our customers, code is just the means to achieve it. Programming algorithms, designing architecture, and following good practices are all tools to help us deliver value. If our customers are not happy with the product, nothing else matters, you won't get any mercy if you show them how beautiful your code is. The same applies to the features we build, adding functionality to the product is not the end goal, work is not done after we push code to production, it ends after we have positive confirmation that the change we made improved the life of users. Teams need to keep learning from mistakes, testing new approaches, and improving on what they build in order to keep delivering consistent value.

Key takeaways:

- Before doing any work, teams need to understand what success means from the business perspective.

- Leverage managers and stakeholders to provide the vision on the expected outcomes for your team.

- In a for-profit company, money is always the ultimate goal, but find proxy metrics if you don't have access to finance data or if your team works on features that do not directly impact revenue.

- Teams should be accountable for their own performance and aways be looking to fix inefficiencies.

- You are not being paid to write code, you are being paid to solve problems; leverage code as a tool to achieve your goals, but don't forget you can also use other tools if they provide a better value.

4.2 Your Success Is the Success of Your Team

We've all heard stories about the lonely hacker who built an amazing new technology that revolutionized the world and these stories are, not always, but sometimes true, at least to some extent. A single engineer can create an innovative piece of software that captures a huge audience, but it's rare for a long-lasting commercial product to be maintained by one single person. Software engineering is majorly a team work and most of its complexity comes from that nature. Solo engineers don't need processes nor documentation, and even good practices are dispensable to some extent, most of the software engineering tooling we have was created to cope with the challenges of having multiple people working on the same codebase. On top of that, most software with a reasonably large audience is way too big and complex to be built by a single person, it's humanly impossible to write and maintain that amount of code. That means it is unlikely that a single engineer working alone is going to be responsible for the long-term success of a product, you'll most likely need a team working together to build any meaningful system that keeps delivering value over time, otherwise it would be easy for competitors to outcompete the product and quickly take over market share.

If the success of the team is the success of the product and you cannot build the product alone, then we can infer that your success is the success of your team. No matter how good of a software engineer you are, you'll need a team doing good work in order to deliver what needs to be done in time. Because of that, it's strategic to treat assisting other people and improving the performance of your team as part of your job. When your teammates become better engineers it makes it more likely that you will deliver value to customers so everyone's odds of being positively evaluated grows and so grows the chances of everyone advancing in their careers. Every time you do an attentive code review, pair program with a teammate, present or recommend a technical content, or give feedback to someone, you are also investing in your own career. It's in your best interest that everyone in the team is happy and performing well, so be intentional in fomenting the environment where other people can flourish and do their best work.

Keep in mind that promoting your teammates won't hinder your protagonism, it will supercharge it. Your teammates, especially folks who are less experienced, will certainly remember the attention and help you give to them. It's natural that peers pull each other up when they grow. A study called "A typology of organizational cultures" by Dr. Ron Westrum found that teams that foster a culture of information flow and trust, perform better. A framework devised from this study became known as *"Westrum organizational culture"* and it defines six principles that influence the effectiveness of teams, they are

- High cooperation: People from multiple functional areas of the organization collaborate to achieve goals.

- Messengers are trained: When people bring in bad news, it's used to fix the problem, not to blame the messenger.

- Risks are shared: There's no single person or group of people with sole ownership of the product or parts of it, everyone shares and owns responsibility when things break.

- Bridging is encouraged: Barriers between people from different areas of the organization are weak and people can easily and directly communicate.

- Failure leads to inquiry, not to individual blaming.

- Novelty is implemented: New ideas are welcome and are given proper attention, not just put aside.

Your organization might directly or indirectly discourage that kind of culture. If that's the case, the best you can do is try to promote these principles and educate people about the benefits.

Another way to empower the team to be successful is by making yourself dispensable. Yes, dispensable, not indispensable. In fact, ideally, your absence should not provoke a noticeable change in the short-term performance of your team. **In a mature and functional team, every person should be able to go on vacation, take time off to recover from illness, and assist their relatives with the peace of mind that it won't have a major impact on the overall performance of the team or lead to an incident.** This is only achievable when everyone becomes dispensable. Being dispensable means that you do your work publicly and that you communicate progress, it means you write good code that is understandable and easy to maintain, it means that you plan and write documentation and that you capacitate other people to execute routines that you are in charge of.

Notice that pretty much every practice we covered in this book is designed to improve how you work collaboratively in a team. Your success is directly tied to the success of your teammates so every time your work empowers them to be more effective or prevents the team from failing you are not only directly contributing to everyone's career but also promoting yours.

Key takeaways:

- Software development is majorly a teamwork, it's rare for a product built by a single person to keep relevant in the long term.

- It's strategic for your career that you help your teammates to grow.

- Promoting a culture of trust and sharing among team members leads to better performance.

- Teams should not be dependent on individuals in order to function, temporary absence should not lead to operation hiccups or incidents.

4.3 Own the Product

Strategic engineers have a broad vision about the company, the team, the product, and how their work impacts business and its customers. In other words, they own the product. Owning the product is not about being an expert in all the knowledge areas required to run a successful business, this is unattainable. Being a designer or product manager requires years of focused study and practice to master. **Owning the product is about being genuinely interested in the success of what you are building beyond the context of software engineering.** It's knowing that you can influence parts of the product and the company that are not directly linked to the job you were hired to do. It's also about having customers in mind at every decision you make and being empathetic to them. It's understanding that your job is to add value to the users, to the company, and to your peers. And it's understanding that there are multiple ways to do it that are not necessarily related to writing software.

As an engineer, one of the best ways to own the product is by being critical of what is asked from you to work on. We've talked about the importance of knowing about the business goals of the product, you should use that information to reflect on the assignment you are given and evaluate if it really matches with the company goals. If you don't think you are working on the right thing, you should feel encouraged to talk to your leadership and question them about the scope of the work or its priority, preferably by also proposing what you think it should be working on instead. When doing this, keep in mind that you don't have the final say on what gets built, so do it in a humble and propositive way. Assume you don't have the full picture and gather more information before you form an opinion. Some leaders will happily provide an explanation on why they made certain decisions but others won't; while that's not ideal, there's not much you can do about it (perhaps not much beyond sharing your feedback, if that's a welcome practice) so don't worry too much. Keep in mind that your goal is to build a successful product, not to be right. After you've gained enough context, you can then present your opinions and explain why you think you should be working on something else. Again, don't worry if your ideas are dismissed, that's part of the job. Companies have a chain of command exactly to deal with the problem of knowing who has the final word, just say thank you and go work on your designated project.

Even if you were assigned to a task that is very well aligned with the business goals, there's still a lot of value in being critical of it. One of the most strategic things you can do is to look for ways to simplify things. Is there any part that can be removed with a low impact on the overall user experience? Is there something that could be left out for a later version? Is there something that is too complicated to implement and that could be done much faster if it was changed a bit? Remember, the sooner you deliver, the sooner you add value to users, and the less code you write, the smaller is the potential for bugs and the simpler it is to maintain the code over time. These same principles apply to the design specs. You might not have a degree in design but you do have experience using digital products. Use that to make suggestions, talk to designers and point out how similar things are done in applications you enjoy using. Try to look at things from the perspective of users:

- What are they trying to accomplish with that functionality?

- Is it easy to accomplish that in the feature you are developing?

- How many clicks and forms does the user need to fill before they can get what they want?

- Is it easy to learn how to use the functionality?

- How could you prevent users from making a mistake?

- What happens if something fails, how can users know about it and fix things without needing to talk to a support person?

- Is there anything that might take longer to run than the user expects?

- How is this break in expectation going to be communicated through the interface?

Answering these questions is commonly a part of product designers' jobs, but engineers can certainly be a part of the design process by identifying issues that designers didn't consider at first or that are linked to technical constraints that only a person with a technical software knowledge could've spotted.

Keep in mind that you can and should contribute to the product with your ideas. Did you think of a functionality that is missing, or do you know of a better way to do something that the product already does? Tell people about it! People have different perspective of the world, you might be seeing something that is not obvious to others. Sharing your ideas is not about hitting the jackpot in one shot, it's about bringing light to something and letting other people form and express their own views about it. Sometimes people will agree, straight on, that your idea is good and it should be executed. But more often, sharing ideas will lead to a collaboration process where they suggest changes to the initial idea resulting in something better. Or even, it will compel the team to think more about the subject which will result in completely different ideas. All of these situations are positive because they all lead to your ultimate goal of adding value to the product. As we've seen, owning the product is a lot about speaking up, communicating and collaborating with your teammates. In the next section we will explore how to be strategic throughout these interactions in order to increase your chances of success.

Key takeaways:

- Owning the product is thinking holistically about the business and knowing that you can participate in all phases of building and running it.

- Don't assume things are immutable, be critical about your assignments and make suggestions about the things you think that can be improved.

- Prioritize simplicity and explain trade-offs to stakeholders so they can better balance cost and benefit.

- The goal is not to have the winning idea, but to spark collaboration that will eventually lead to a better product.

4.4 Collaborate

Knowing the importance of collaboration to the success of a team, you should treat it as a key aspect of your work as an engineer. That means that, once again, you should be very intentional and strategic when interacting with your peers. Every meeting, document, chat, code review, or pair programming session should be viewed as an opportunity to help individuals grow, to share knowledge, and even to improve team morale. These seemingly small interactions add up and can make a big difference in the team's overall performance. It's not surprising that communication is key to successful collaboration. The way you approach your teammates during these moments is decisive to the effectiveness of your actions. You might have all the knowledge in the world, but if you can't communicate your ideas to your teammates, you are going to significantly reduce the potential impact of your work.

The first thing to understand is that collaboration is only effective if it's positive to all parts involved. If you turn collaboration opportunities into an argument with the goal of winning over someone, you automatically lose the majority of the benefits of that interaction. **Everyone in the team should be seeking the success of the product, which should be above**

the success of any individual. If you are not willing to accept that other people's ideas can be better than yours or that they can improve on what you originally suggested, it means that you are prioritizing something else other than the success of the product. That kind of behavior is unproductive, especially if what you are prioritizing is your ego. Even when you have a strong opinion and think that everyone else is wrong, it's not strategic to assume an inflexible position. Your goal is to get the ideas you believe in picked and executed by the team, so you have to do what will most likely lead to that outcome. If you are harsh and derogatory, people will get defensive and you won't achieve your goal. Instead, keep a positive and constructive attitude, slowly lead peers to understand your reasoning and get them to agree with you topic by topic. People are more likely to be receptive to your ideas if they also feel that you are receptive to theirs. Explicitly highlight the things you liked about their contributions and make them feel heard and considered. Making concessions on details that you judge secondary is also a great strategy. By doing that, you make others part of the solution, bringing in allies to your side. It's a small toll you pay to get people onboard with your ideas. Remember: It's only collaboration if it generates a net positive to everyone involved. If you use collaboration opportunities to spit out opinions with no regard for other people, it has the complete opposite effect. It's detrimental to your peers, to customers, to the product, and to your career.

How you present your ideas also matters a lot; communication is a skill that can be learned and that needs practice to be mastered. **When people don't understand what you are saying, the burden of improving the communication is yours, not theirs.** Experiment with different forms of communication, perhaps you are more effective when you do some prior preparation, or when you use visual aids such as a presentation or even screen share the code you are debating. You can experiment with different strategies of presenting your ideas. For instance, you can try first giving a quick overview of the topic before diving into detailed items. Try first presenting your end goal before explaining the steps that will lead to it, or try investing more time explaining your reasoning before jumping to conclusions. The success rate of techniques will vary depending on who's communicating, who's the audience, and what is the context, so you need to experiment with different approaches. Practice until you discover what works best for you, and adapt your strategy accordingly. In fact, even factor in that the people you are communicating with might be having a bad day, or that they are really focused on something else at the moment. That way you might decide that is more likely to get your point across if you move a meeting to some other time, make it shorter or even replace it with an email. At the end of the day, what matters is that you get your point across.

Collaboration is not a one-time thing, it happens over extended periods and every interaction counts toward a long-term successful outcome. Remember that you are dealing with human beings and that not everything is about efficiency. Cultivating a healthy relationship with coworkers beyond your strict work activities can lead to a more integrated and collaborative team. Build stronger connections with people by chatting about non-work topics, ask questions about them and demonstrate interest in their lives. If they are willing to share, don't be afraid to share things about yourself too. How people perceive you also matters, no one likes working with arrogant people, exercise humbleness, be assertive but leave space for doubt, explicitly differentiate what are the facts and what is your opinion, encourage people to speak up in case they don't agree with you. If you don't know about something don't be afraid to ask for context, showing vulnerability leads to more trustful relationships. Assume good intentions, there's no gain in making enemies. Strictly speaking, there's no strategic benefit in mistreating people or making their lives harder, even if you two didn't hit it off. Avoid taking things personally; in most cases, people are just trying to do what they believe to be the right thing. Everyone has their own professional objectives and interests in mind so it's natural that sometimes there will be conflict. Control your impulses, try to keep cool and avoid escalating the situation. The more allies you have among your teammates, the greater are your chances of being successful.

Don't be a source of noise to your managers. As mentioned before, being open and explicit about your opinions is a positive trait in a team, but overdoing that can be harmful. No one likes to work with a person who's constantly complaining about the same things over and over. Do your best to bring attention to the things you consider important but also learn to stop once you notice people do not agree with you. If your manager tells you that they are not going to make your issue a priority at the moment or simply downplays the importance of it, there's no point in insisting on it every time you meet. Back off for a while and bring the topic up again sometime later when priorities have changed, or when you notice there's a higher risk to it than it had before. Keep in mind that it's not your manager's job to solve your problems. They are certainly there to do whatever they can to enable the team to do their best work but they have ownership to choose what gets prioritized. **Practice finding other paths to get what you want, perhaps there's someone else in the company that can help you out, or you can try mobilizing people in the team to vouch for you.** In some situations it's better to just accept things are not going to happen the way you want. Your idea might not be aligned with the company strategy and that's just the way things are, learn to accept defeat and move on without letting it bother you too much. Be careful with topics that might be sensitive so you don't put your managers and peers in a tough position. Perhaps a meeting with everyone in the team is not the best place to bring up certain topics. Instead, first chat privately with your leader and ask if you can take the issue openly to the team. As usual, form is important. Reframe complaints as propositions and suggestions, that way you are more likely to get your point across and the issue resolved than when you sound grumpy.

Finally, don't let detractors hinder the success of the team, use your influence to talk to people and convert detractors into allies. Offer assistance where you can help, direct people into using the company policies and tools that might get them back on track. In case you don't feel capable of dealing with a situation or if your efforts are not yielding results, don't hesitate to report to your leadership. When reporting, don't use personal opinions and feelings about the person. Be direct and professional, focus on the practical actions that you believe to be affecting the team. Your goal should be to fix the issue and there are many ways to achieve that, if it's out of your control, do your part and leave the decision to who's in charge of it.

Key takeaways:

- If you are not the one in charge of making the final decision, communication and collaboration are the tools you have to have your ideas picked.

- Hear what people have to say and make them allies by acknowledging their contributions.

- If people are not hearing what you say, consider that you might not be properly communicating, try saying things differently and explore other forms of communication until you find what works best for you.

- For a happier and more effective team, build meaningful relationships with your colleagues.

- Don't insist on approaches that are not working, look for alternative ways to get what you want and know when to back off.

4.5 Block Noise and Keep Focus

While there are uncountable benefits to collaborating in a group, it's inevitable that there will be distractions. People easily lose their focus and get hung up on the wrong things. A single comment is sometimes enough to get the whole team wasting time on parallel discussions and even to derail major delivery goals, leading to investment on things that don't add value to the product and delays shipping (this is known as "bikeshedding"). It's impossible to prevent these distractions from happening so the challenge is learning how to reduce its impact and how to keep your individual effectiveness as an engineer despite the chaos. **Noise is everything that directly or indirectly, doesn't contribute to the business, product, or team objectives, especially when done at inappropriate moments.** Strategic engineers keep their eyes on the goal, consciously avoiding focus traps and help steer their team's attention and time investment in the right direction.

In a team there should be space for everyone's opinions. People should be able to speak and raise their hands to expose what they have in mind, as long as it's done in a respectful and professional manner. However that doesn't mean any space is an open stand for them to bring in any of their ideas. There is a proper time, place, and way for things to be discussed in order to make communication effective and keep the team productive. As we discussed in the first chapter, meetings should have a predefined agenda, which doesn't mean absolutely no sidetrack is allowed. If there's some parallel topic that needs discussing, it's ok to squeeze it in between the planned agenda, but it's important to keep a close watch on the time. That period was reserved to achieve some objective or reach a certain decision and there's usually people depending on its outcomes. If you notice that parallel topics are deviating too much focus, it's ok to bring that to the attention of participants so you can get back on track. Propose scheduling another dedicated meeting to discuss that matter or take it asynchronously. Equally, if you have a question that is not directly related to the meeting topic, wait to bring it up at the end of the meeting if there's some time left so you don't derail focus.

Finding the right time to discuss things is important. Things that are going to happen far in the future sometimes require a lot of preparation in advance, but at the same time, discussing things too soon often means there's going to be a lot of speculation on information that is still incomplete or missing and that you might be drawing scenarios that are far from reality when things come to be. If you notice that people are investing too much time discussing topics that could be decided later on, when there's more data available, don't hesitate to propose to wait a little more and schedule another moment to close the matter. **Delaying precipitated discussions can reduce the anxiety of overthinking things and keep the conversation more assertive and based on reliable information.**

A situation where there's usually a lot of noise is during incidents and crises. In these situations, people tend to get overwhelmed by the pressure to fix things and either end up spending effort on the wrong initiatives or simply become paralyzed. Without someone to steer focus, chaos tends to grow, leading the team to spin in circles and delaying action. Keeping calm during these situations is key and is something that you should actively pursue. Practice blocking out the noise so you can think strategically about what you need to do. In the first moment, all your energy must be focused on mitigating the damage; it doesn't matter what broke or who's responsible, do whatever you can to reduce the impacts of the problem. Distinguish the problem from the symptoms. Unless you already know what the problem is and how to fix it fast, start by working on the symptoms. Depending on the situation, reducing damage might mean bringing the whole system down, isolating the problem by turning off a feature while allowing other parts of the system to keep working, or even issuing an announcement to affected parties. The goal is to reduce pressure to allow the team to work in a more stable environment where they can properly identify root causes and design the adequate solutions. Pressure makes complex decisions even riskier so you want to be in a position where you have more time to plan and assess the situation before investing on the actual solution to the problem. One other important tip related to incidents is learning to read the room. There are situations, especially when you don't have enough context, where it's better to step back so you don't become a source of noise to other people. If this is the case, make yourself available and wait until your assistance is requested. Or perhaps you can do your own investigation alone and just report back in case you find something worth sharing.

Another common source of noise is conflict between team members. These situations are harder to deal with because they might involve personal issues and, depending on the case, getting involved might be quite tricky. Unfortunately, this kind of conflict can affect team performance so, if you know the parts and feel comfortable, it might be a good idea to jump in and help mediate the issue in order to restore team harmony. If you don't feel comfortable and the situation seems to be escalating, it might be a good idea to get help from your leadership or use the proper company channels to get some guidance on what to do. If you find yourself in a conflict with a teammate, do your best to reflect on the situation and evaluate what is the outcome you expect from it. Try to think straight and leave part of the feelings aside, think strategically if there's any positive outcome possible and if they would surpass the negative side effects. If you conclude that it's not really worth it, don't be ashamed, just let it go or even apologize if that would disarm the situation. Having that level of self-control is of course not easy, but you can practice by avoiding being reactive and giving yourself time to think strategically about what you expect from the situation and what action would lead to the best outcome for yourself and to the team.

Key takeaways:

- Distractions are everywhere, know what are your goals and help the team stay on the right track to achieving them.

- Find the appropriate moment to bring up the things you want to share in order to avoid disrupting other discussions.

- It's unproductive to waste time speculating about things that can be decided later on when more information is available.

- Keep calm during incidents, first focus on stabilizing the situations so you can reduce pressure and think clearly.

- Help in disarming conflicts and only engage on the ones that are worth your time and that can generate positive outcomes for the team.

4.6 Disagree and Commit

Conflict, when properly managed within the boundaries of professional behavior, is a powerhouse for evolution. When engineers with different ideas and points of view work together collaboratively, the result is usually a more robust product that is resilient to a broader set of risks. It's also more likely to deliver value because it has more eyes validating it's going to do what it's expected to do. Unfortunately, consensus is a scarce asset in the real world and so is the time available for engineers to keep battling over their personal opinions. It's not reasonable to expect everyone to completely agree on every project decision, so it's important that people learn to identify when discussions stop being productive and turn into blockers of progress. In the end, the ultimate test for any idea is making it a reality, observing how it performs, learning from the results and improving it, or throwing it away in favor of something else. **Disagree and commit is a state of mind where a person truly embraces a decision they are not in full agreement with because they understand that, sometimes, it's more important to make a decision and put it to the test than it is to win an argument.**

The ability to disagree and move forward with a decision is a basic skill to anyone working in a group. Without it, nothing would ever get done because people would be constantly wasting time on endless discussions. During a conflict, most people are capable of disagreeing and moving on with their lives leaving the situation unsettled. "Disagreeing" is the part of "disagree and commit" that everyone gets and can perform reasonably well, but "committing" is not always fully understood or put in practice. Committing goes beyond not complaining about the decision, it is really internalizing and believing in the decision that was made. It means doing your best to make that plan successful, rooting for it, and feeling an integral part of the outcome of it even when you previously were explicitly against it or preferred to go in another direction. This is a difference that might seem too subtle or even irrelevant because it's effectively just a small change in how you face the situation, but when working in a group it can make a real impact on the outcome. People are usually happier and form a greater sense of collectiveness when they are working in a team where everyone is supportive to group decisions.

Given that the success of the product is the goal and that a decision was already made, the only strategy that can maximize results is to fully embrace the decision. It's already settled that the team is going to invest their time and effort in that direction, so not being supportive of it can, at best, diminish the chances of it succeeding and the investment going to waste. Even when you disagree with the group, it's beneficial to yourself to promote and advocate for the collective decision. The best strategy will always be to behave as if you truly believed in that decision, doing good work and helping your teammates to thrive. Detractors mine the chances of an idea from possibly working, sabotaging experimentation and even leading the team to draw the wrong conclusions about a solution that could've been positive for the product. So first commit to the strategy, do your best (including communicating risks you observe), wait to see how it performs and in case it fails, you can then influence the team to try something else. **Remember that either the whole team is successful or no one is, proving people wrong does not make you successful.**

Disagreeing and committing does not mean you don't fight for your ideas once someone opposes it, even when that comes from your leadership. As we talked before, generating friction is positive and usually leads to better results so you should definitely sustain your opinions and use everything in your power to convince people of your points. What is important is that you don't overshoot and learn when it's time to stop. Be attentive to what your teammates are saying against your proposition and especially how they are saying it. Leaders are not always going to explicitly say that they've already made a decision, they know people perform better when they are on board. That means sometimes they are promoting discussions just to help their team feel engaged in the cause, not because they are really willing to change their mind. Pay attention to that and once you notice the decision has been made, stop insisting and start planning how you are going to help bring that vision to life with your team. Finally, learn to pick your battles. You are not always going to win so focus on the things you judge more important, do your best to improve on the ideas you don't fully agree with and identify when fighting is not worth it. If this is the case, accept and commit to the group decision.

Key takeaways:

- Disagree and commit requires that you fully embrace the decisions by doing your best to make it successful despite your disbelief.

- Once a decision has been made the most strategic thing you can do is to fully support it, it's in your best interest that it works because if it fails it's bad for everyone.

- Pick your battles, fight for the things you really consider important and avoid wasting energy on the things that are not worthy.

4.7 Master Giving Feedback

Giving feedback is one of the most powerful tools for teamwork. It is a great way for you to contribute to your teammates' growth and impact the long-term success of the team. These small and continuous course corrections make a big difference in anyone's personal career and can help quickly address issues that could cause severe damage if left unattended. In a healthy team, feedback should be part of everyone's routine and happen between every team member regardless of hierarchy or level of experience. Junior engineers do have relevant contributions to make to senior folk. Building a culture of feedback in a team is not easy, it requires an intentional effort from everyone before it picks up momentum and becomes natural. Even if that's not something your team already does, you can start practicing yourself and show people the benefits of it. Although the concept of giving feedback is easy to understand, you can greatly improve its effectiveness with small adjustments in the form you do it and by having the right mindset and expectations about it.

A common misconception when thinking about feedback is only considering constructive feedback. Although constructive feedback is certainly what yields the most significant results, giving positive feedback also plays an important role. **With constructive feedback you provide information about the behaviors you'd like changed but there's also value in expliciting things you want to keep happening, so providing positive feedback prevents things that are good from stop happening.** It also has a significant impact on a team's culture, by making feedback moments lighter and removing some of the negative stigma of it. That way when someone says they want to give feedback people don't have to assume they made a mistake, thus reducing some of the anxiety from the process. Feedback should not be a burden, it should be a light and enriching experience for both parties. Positive or constructive, when feedback is properly handled it always has a positive outcome. When giving feedback, your intentions should always be to help someone to improve on something, not to drop a bomb on their hands and let them handle it by themselves.

With a few basic tactics you can greatly improve the quality of your feedback. First of all, give it the importance it deserves by preparing for it. Reserve a few minutes to think and write down what you want to say. A few sentences listed in bullet points to use as a guide is usually enough.

If you are worried that you might not deliver the message properly or forget something, it might be worth it to actually write full sentences that you can just read aloud. Reading during a feedback meeting might make things sound too mechanical and remove the personal touch that is important for feedback, so use it as a way to practice until you get comfortable enough with the process to not need it. One key advantage of writing things down while preparing to give feedback is that you can send it asynchronously to the person after the meeting, thus giving one more tool to help them understand the message. Use this preparation moment to refine the message you want to convey, try to really identify the key points you want to communicate and how you are going to express them in a clear and concise way. To help with that, try to be specific and avoid using broad or generic affirmations. Back your ideas with examples of actions the person did that led to the issue. Take the opportunity to review your biases: are you being fair? Are your expectations well aligned with that person's job title and experience level? Reflect among the things you listed which are critical and which are less important. Check if you are only touching on points that the person can actually change, and that all topics are work related. Make sure to be explicit about priorities when you are giving feedback, people can usually work on two or three things at a time, so just dropping a bucket of ideas won't help them fix what matters the most first.

Feedback represents the point of view of the person who is giving it, it should be based on facts but will always be molded by one's personal perspective. Don't forget that what you are saying is just your perspective of the facts, not an absolute truth. Also don't just assume people have the same view of the world as yourself. Explain why you consider the situation an issue and the impact you are observing. The person receiving the feedback is not obligated to agree with you and sometimes that can make them get into a defensive stance. If that happens, don't try to respond, just reinstate that you are only giving your perspective on the subject and move on; feedback is not a moment for heated arguments. Using expressions that explicitly highlight that "biased" nature of feedback is also a great technique to avoid getting into conflict. Instead of just saying "what you did was wrong," try to use expressions like "In my opinion ...," "the way I see it ...," or "my understanding of the situation is ..." Talking about how things affected yourself can also help, for example, you can say: "it made me anxious to see things were not done properly," "I felt sad by the way you expressed yourself in that meeting," or "it worries me when you forget about the things we agreed on." **Often, it is less important to decide what did or did not happen and instead focus on how it was perceived and what can be done to change that perception.**

Besides giving a perspective of the facts, good constructive feedback should also communicate what changes are expected. Being explicit about that is important because even when people agree on what the problem is, it's possible that they have different ideas about what is the right solution to it. By saying how you expect the problem to be fixed you are providing tools to help the person receiving the feedback. Discussing solutions is also another mechanism to validate if the message was properly transmitted and understood.

As we've seen multiple times over this book, the form of your communication matters. Feedback should be assertive. Softening the message is a risky approach and usually results in miscommunication. For years in my career I thought that providing good explanations and being clear was enough for giving good feedback. I noticed that despite my effort, some people would not fully grasp the importance of what I was saying and would keep going back to the same issues. Studying about feedback and experimenting I learned that tone has an essential role in this kind of communication. If something is critical, it's not enough to state that it's critical, your tone also needs to convey it. I started noticing that the feedback where I maintained a firm tone and I was more assertive were more effective, and that this was beneficial for everyone because it meant people would better understand the importance of what I was saying and improve faster.

Being direct and using a professional tone is in most times the most effective way to communicate. At the same time, feel free to leverage your relationship with people to adapt the tone. If you know that the person is more sensitive, perhaps you can use a calming tone to help the conversation to run more smoothly. The opposite also happens, some people don't react unless they notice it's a critical issue, if that's the case, it's ok to be a bit more direct and incisive. Remember that your goal is to improve things, so be intentional and use the strategy that is most likely to generate the desired outcome.

Key takeaways:

- Prepare and practice giving feedback to improve your technique.

- Be kind and empathetic, but don't refrain from being assertive.

- It's ok if people don't agree with your feedback.

- Use all the tools you have to help get your point across effectively.

4.8 Master Receiving Feedback

Just like when you are giving feedback, there are things you can do to improve how you receive feedback. At first sight, it might seem strange to think that the person receiving feedback has to do anything other than hearing what others have to say. But the rationale behind improving on how you receive feedback lies in recognizing the importance of it in your career growth and understanding that giving feedback is hard for everyone. **It's in your best interest to make it a good experience for people to give you feedback so they are willing to do it often and are comfortable talking about difficult topics.**

The first thing to keep in mind about receiving feedback is internalizing the right mindset. Feedback is a tool for visibility, it is an opportunity to learn about something that you can improve in your behavior or in the way you do your job. The opposite of not receiving feedback is keeping on failing without ever knowing about it until things irreversibly break. It's also essential not to treat feedback as a direct attack on yourself. The fact that you failed on something does not mean you are intrinsically incompetent, it just means there's something you can improve in the way you are doing your job, and now that you know about it, you can deliberately make the appropriate changes to improve. **Consider it a privilege that your teammates care about you and are willing to invest their time helping you to get better at your job and be thankful for it.**

Another important shift is to stop wasting time on trying to agree on what or how things happened and focus on how things were perceived by the person addressing you. It doesn't matter if you were right or wrong, someone perceived it as negative, so at the very least you can change your behavior so that it will be perceived more positively the next time. When you adopt these changes in perspective it becomes a lot lighter and easier for you and for the other person giving you feedback to handle this delicate interaction.

Ask for feedback both from your peers and your leaders. In teams that do not yet have a strong feedback culture, the natural tendency is that only leaders give feedback to their subordinates. Until people develop a regular habit of giving feedback, you can accelerate that process by directly asking for feedback from the people you interact with. Being specific about what you want feedback about helps a lot in the quality of the information you will get from people; ask things like "can you give me feedback on how I handled X situation?" When you don't specify, people will usually bring up generic comments that are less helpful.

There are many small behavior tweaks that can facilitate feedback sessions. For instance, you should pay attention to your body posture and use positive face expressions that indicate you are receptive to the things being said or at least try to stay neutral. Avoiding responding right away is also helpful, first listen to what the person has to say and use that moment strategically to collect more information, do your best to fill in gaps of information, and to make sure you understand what is the problem and how it affected others. It's ok to give your perspective, but in these situations, it's possible that it will sound like you are trying to justify yourself, so if you want to do that, make it explicit that you are not contesting the feedback. Most importantly, **don't ever engage in an argument; if you notice things are heating up, take a step back and assume a listening posture.** If you feel the feedback is too generic and are having difficulty relating to it, you can ask the person to provide some practical examples. The same goes if you are not sure what you can do to improve; you can ask if the person has a suggestion.

It's a good idea to write things down during the conversation if you can do it without losing concentration, that way you reduce the risk of forgetting something. Otherwise you can also spend a few minutes after the session writing notes, try to do it as soon as possible so you have a fresh take. Ending the session by summarizing the top items is also a great way to recap and ensure you got all the main points. Don't forget to show gratitude and thank the person for taking the time to give you feedback. In a later moment, use your notes to reflect on the things you learned; if you notice something is missing or if you have any extra questions, don't hesitate to schedule a new session or ask asynchronously. Once you are confident you understand the situation, define an action plan with the things you are going to do to address the main issues. In some situations, especially when the feedback is coming from a direct leader, you might want to present your plan so it can be validated. In that case, don't forget to keep regular reports about your progress and ask for feedback on them. Having someone with an external point of view who you can discuss with can be extremely useful during this process.

Be grateful that people feel comfortable being vulnerable with you, receiving honest feedback is a privilege. Do your best to enhance the experience of the people giving feedback to you and don't expect to agree with everything you are told. Use the opportunity to gather as much information as you can, reflect on what you consider important and make an improvement plan. Remember that more is better, don't hesitate to explicitly and regularly ask for feedback and seek a second opinion if you feel it's going to be beneficial to hear someone else's take.

Key takeaways:

- Receiving feedback is something to be grateful about, it's an opportunity to reflect on how you can improve.

- Make it easy for others to give you feedback so they are comfortable doing it regularly.

- You don't need to agree with the feedback you receive, reflect and act on what you consider relevant.

- Learning about how things were perceived is more important than agreeing on what actually happened.

- Periodically ask for feedback from the people around you; for better results, be specific about the things you want feedback about.

4.9 References and Further Reading

- "Accelerate: The Science of Lean Software and DevOps: Building and Scaling High Performing Technology Organizations" book by Nicole Forsgren, Jez Humble, Gene Kim

- "The SPACE of Developer Productivity" by Nicole Forsgren, Margaret-Anne Storey, Chandra Maddila, Thomas Zimmermann, Brian Houck, and Jenna Butler https://queue.acm.org/detail.cfm?id=3454124

- "Are you an Elite DevOps performer? Find out with the Four Keys Project" by Dina Graves Portman https://cloud.google.com/blog/products/devops-sre/using-the-four-keys-to-measure-your-devops-performance

- "DevOps capabilities" https://cloud.google.com/architecture/devops?hl=en

Conclusion

The ideas in this book were developed throughout my career as a software engineer by reading books and blog posts, attending conferences, watching live and recorded talks, but especially by sharing experiences with teammates and fellow engineers, observing people's behavior, and doing my own experimentations. As the co-founder of a software development shop that specializes in delivering tailor-made products to clients, it was essential that I could pass on the things I learned to everyone in my team so we could consolidate our practices, improve the quality of our work and grow as a company. I wrote internal documents and processes, published posts in our internal communications tools and on the public company blog, sent memos, gave presentations, promoted discussions during company meetings, and mentored people. I have no doubt about the positive impact these actions had on Vinta's business, to the career of the people who work with us and to our clients.

One of my personal goals for this book was to consolidate some of these insights I've had in my professional journey so that others could join into the core discussion: how can we be better software engineers? It was never my goal to write a complete guide on the topics I've brought in, but rather to provide insights on improvements engineers can make in order to be more effective in their work. Unfortunately, this particular medium of communication doesn't allow you to directly reply back to me with your personal views, but I hope the book enticed you to reflect on your day-to-day practices [a "self-discussion" if you may], and that perhaps it sparked (or will soon spark) new discussions among you and your teammates. You can also keep it at arm's-length for consultation and point teammates to specific sections that can help them with their work and career challenges.

© Filipe Ximenes 2024
F. Ximenes, *Strategic Software Engineering*, https://doi.org/10.1007/979-8-8688-0995-8

Finally, don't get hung up on doing exactly what is suggested in the chapters. I encourage you to try the ideas in this book as they are presented as much as I encourage you to learn from the results and make adaptations that might lead to better outcomes in your particular context. As long as you are communicating and collaborating with the people around you, testing new ideas can only lead to better results in the long term.

Index